Islam

the choice of

Thinking Women

Ismail Adam Patel

Ta-Ha Publishers Ltd.
1 Wynne Road
London SW9 0BB
United Kingdom

Published in Al-Oola 1418 AH/September 1997 CE by

Ta-Ha Publishers Ltd.
1 Wynne Road
London SW9 0BB
website:http://www.taha.co.uk/
email: sales@taha.co.uk

Edited by : Huda Khattab

British Library Cataloguing in Publication
Catalogue Record for this Publication Available from The
British Library

RePrinted 1999

ISBN 1 897940 63 7

Printed and Bound by- De-Luxe Printers,
London NW10 7NR.
website: http://www.de-luxe.com

بِسْمِ اللهِ الرَّحْمٰنِ الرَّحِيمِ

IN THE NAME OF ALLAH, MOST GRACIOUS, MOST MERCIFUL

And among His signs is this, that He created for you mates from among yourselves, that you may dwell in tranquillity with them, and He has put love and mercy between your (hearts) : Verily in that are signs for those who reflect.

And among His signs is the creation of the heavens and the earth, and the variations in your languages and your colours: Verily in that are signs for those who know.

[Ar-Rum 30:21,22]

Contents

I

WOMAN – A CROSS CULTURE PERSPECTIVE

II

SOCIAL POSITION OF 'WESTERN WOMEN' TODAY

III

WOMEN IN ISLAM

IV

THE FEMINIST MOVEMENT

ACKNOWLEDGEMENT

My debt to my Creator, whose Bounties and Mercies I cannot begin to glorify even if *'all the Worlds water were provided as ink for me and wood as scribe to praise His Glory'*. It is only through His Mercies that my soul survives and enjoys.

This book has been made possible by the efforts, encouragement's and duas of many. I am particularly grateful to: Mufti Fahem Mayat (Principal, Madraasa Islamia, Batley, England) whose amendments from Islamic jurisprudence point of view, especially in chapter 3 has been invaluable. Professor Sheikh Awadalla Youssef's (The Rector, The Open School For Arabic and Islamic Studies, Manchester, England) advice to include statistics from throughout the World on the status of women has no doubt given the book a new dimension. Mufti Zubair Bayat's (Principal, Zakariyya Muslim School, Stanger, South Africa) great effort in bringing the book with the literary norms is greatly appreciated. Sheikh Muhammad Saleem Dhorat's (Editor Riyaadh ul Jannah & Imam Masjida Noor, Leicester, England) continual encouragement has been a source of inspiration. Sheikh Ibrahim Iqbal Patel's (Ilmi Publication) guidance on publication has also been invaluable. I am also grateful to Mufti Muhammad Taqi Usmani (Justice, Supreme Court of Pakistan, Karachi, Pakistan) for his encouraging words and duas.

I have been very fortunate to have had the access to the talents of such great scholars of Islam, may their efforts be rewarded by Allah subhana wata'ala – Ameen.

I am also grateful to sister Huda Khattab (Ontario, Canada) who edited the original 'raw' manuscript, Dr. Ali Dhariwala and Ta Ha for publication.

Last but not least, there are off course my children, Mariam and Huzayfa, wife and family who allowed me the freedom, peace and tranquillity to write in the house, after working hours. No doubt there have been many others who have worked earnestly to make this publication possible and for all I pray – Allah subhana wata'ala reward them abundantly – Ameen.

FORWARD

Perusing through the script of '*Islam The choice of Thinking Women*' has been an exciting learning experience for myself. I feel honoured to write a forward for Br. Ismail.

There is no doubt that the issue of the status of woman in Islam is among the most abused and most worn out propaganda tool in the hands of the Islamaphobe lobby worldwide. Their barrage of abuse against Islam on this score has resulted in great confusion in the minds of people, including unfortunately, some Muslims. The unreasonable and sometimes paranoiac extent to which they have stooped to hype up public opinion against Islamic Hijab, a symbol of modesty and dignity in Muslim female garb, can be understood from the caption of a photograph in one weekly journal of International circulation which carries the photograph of a Muslim woman donning a veil as 'The veiled threat of Islam!'.

In a climate where such hostility exists against the viewpoint of Islam on the status of woman, it is of absolute necessity that the distortions and confusion created by the Western media be rectified in a clear, sober, captivating and intellectual fashion. Another essential element is to present the facts in a manner that is understood and appreciated even by unbiased non-Muslims seeking the truth. At least this would repair some of the damage done to the good name of Islam by those hell-bent on vilifying it by any means.

This book sets out to achieve some of the above points. The author has taken great trouble to explain the pre-Islamic status of women from direct sources. Thereafter, the status of women in Islam is explored from various angles. Furthermore, present day developments on woman's rights and the 'shifting sand' stand of feminism in this matter is analysed in some detail. The fragmentation of the feminist movement and it's diverse and extreme viewpoints are exposed. The mind boggling confusion in their camps becomes manifest. Their alleged claims of representing womankind as a whole is exploded.

It is necessary for all thinking women to make an informed choice of the way of life they wish to adopt. This book will assist them in their choice – Insha Allah. It will equip justice loving persons with sound arguments to counter the deluge of falsehood and damaging propaganda pervading the media of the world on this subject.

This book will make an ideal gift for all, Muslim and non-Muslims alike. May Allah accept this work in His infinite mercy and make it a means of guidance for the honest seekers of truth from all denominations. May He reward the author with a befitting reward and accept from him monumental works of Islam – Ameen.

Mufti Zubair Bayat
Principal, Zakariyya School, Stanger, South Africa.

INTRODUCTION

It has been through Allah's Mercies and Blessings that I have been able to complete this book, which I began in Sha'ban 1414 AH (February 1994). I am a Muslim, a fact which I must make clear to the reader from the outset, for this is a book with an objective, to clarify what is arguably the most frequently discussed aspect of my faith: the position of women in Islam. In doing so, I wish to take this matter beyond the usual defence of Islam and seek a positive understanding of why women are embracing Islam in increasing numbers. I will also examine the role of feminism in today's world.

For far too long, Muslims have had to put up with the criticism, based on ignorance, that their faith is "irrational in the modern age". Islam, and Muslim women in particular, continue to be subjected to ridicule and mockery throughout the Western world. In all of this the media play a key role in orchestrating misinformation, slander and downright lies about Islam.

Despite the almost superhuman efforts to break the spirit of Islam in Muslims, this faith remains the fastest-growing religion in the world. In Europe and North America the progress of Islam is well documented in census reports. Moreover, it is reported that out of every ten "new" Muslims, seven are women.[1] Speculation abounds as to why individuals - especially women - accept Islam when they have been bombarded, courtesy of the Western media, with inaccurate and demeaning "information" about the faith. The simple fact remains that when the light of truth shines into the soul, the mind and heart are opened and every aspect of the human being submits to the Creator of the Universe. This transformation suppresses materialistic, worldly desires, and brings about serenity, contentment, and inner peace.

A common error is the assumption that Islam is merely a "religion", in the sense that it defines belief in God, or prescribes certain acts of worship to be performed or rules to be complied with. In fact, Islam is much more than a "religion" in this narrow sense. It is a *deen*, a

---

[1] *The Times*, London, 7 January 1994.

complete way of life which encompasses every aspect of human life, from the "religious" to the social, economical, medical and political.

The core of Islam is *Tawhid*. No matter how uneducated, remote or isolated a Muslim may be, *Tawhid* is the focus of his or her belief. This firm and unequivocal belief in the absolute uniqueness of Allah, the Lord and Creator of all, is the very essence of Islam. Belief in *Tawhid* is to affirm that there is only One Creator and Sustainer Who deserves to be worshipped and obeyed. Our belief is clear:

> Say: He is Allah, the One and Only; Allah, the Eternal, Absolute; He begets not, nor is He begotten; And there is none like unto Him.
>
> *[al-Ikhlas 112:1-4]*

> Allah is He, other than Whom there is no other god - Who knows (all things) both secret and open; He, Most Gracious, Most Merciful.
>
> Allah is He, other than Whom there is no other god - the Sovereign, the Holy One, the Source of Peace (and Perfection), the Guardian of Faith, the Preserver of Safety, the Exalted in Might, the Irresistible, the Supreme: Glory to Allah! (High is He) above the partners they attribute to Him. He is Allah, the Evolver, the Bestower of Forms (or Colours). To Him belong the Most Beautiful Names: whatever is in the heavens and on earth, declares His Praises and Glory, and He is the Exalted in Might, the Wise.
>
> *[al-Hashr 59:22-24]*

> Allah! There is no god but He - the Living, the Self-subsisting, Eternal. No slumber can seize Him nor sleep. His are all things in the heavens and on earth. Who is there that can intercede in His presence except as He permits? He knows what (appears to His creatures as) Before or After or Behind them. Nor shall they compass aught of His knowledge except as He wills. His Throne extends

over the heavens and the earth, and He feels no
fatigue in guarding and preserving them for He is
the Most High, the Supreme (in glory).

[al-Baqarah 2:255]

The individual's voluntary submission to Allah through sincere
belief in *Tawhid* brings emancipation from worldly, materialistic
bonds, and raises the Muslim, the one who submits to the will of
Allah, to a higher level. This submission liberates individuals from
all false worship, whether it be of the occult, of money, of fortune-
telling, of material gods, of "saints", of those who pretentiously claim
to be intermediaries acting on behalf of God, of self-conceit and of
arrogance. This submission also frees human beings from the burden
of social and peer pressure, as the Muslim submits to the will of
Allah, and to nothing and no-one else. It provides a person with
positive identity and definite position in relation to the rest of creation
and to other human beings. Moreover, it grants him or her direct
access to Allah, the Creator of all.

A Muslim who has freely accepted Islam thus submits to the will
of Allah and obeys His commandments. Human beings know about
these commandments through *Risalah* (Prophethood): Allah has sent
His Guidance through chosen people whom we call Prophets or
Messengers, who conveyed Allah's message to their fellow humans.
The chain of *Risalah* began with Adam and continued through
numerous Prophets including Noah, Abraham, Ishmael, Isaac, Jacob,
Joseph, Moses and Jesus, culminating in the Prophethood of
Muhammad (may peace be upon all the Prophets and Messengers of
Allah). Some Prophets were given books of guidance, such as the
Tawrat (Torah) of Moses, the *Injeel* (Gospel) of Jesus and the Qur'an
brought by Muhammad ﷺ.[1] The Qur'an is the final book of guidance
revealed by Allah to mankind, and it supersedes all previous scriptures
which by admission of their adherents, as is well known, have been
altered and distorted over the centuries. The Qur'an is the only
scripture that has remained in its original form since its revelation
fourteen hundred years ago. The Holy Qur'an itself states:

---

[1] Peace and blessing of Allah be upon the Prophet.

Alif, Lam, Mim. Allah! There is no god but He -
the Living, the Self-subsisting, Eternal.

It is He Who sent down to you (step by step) in
truth, the Book, confirming what went before it;
and He sent down the Law (of Moses) and the
Gospel (of Jesus) Before this, as a guide to
mankind, and He sent down the Criterion (of
judgement between right and wrong). Then those
who reject faith in the Signs of Allah will suffer
the severest penalty, and Allah is Exalted in Might,
Lord of Retribution.

From Allah, verily nothing is hidden on earth or
in the heavens. He it is Who shapes you in the
wombs as He pleases. There is no god but He, the
Exalted in Might, the Wise.

[Al 'Imran 3:1-6]

The faith of Islam as we know it today (for it must be borne in
mind that all the Prophets taught submission to the will of Allah, or
Islam) is derived from the Holy Qur'an and the teachings, examples
and practices of Allah's final Messenger, Prophet Muhammad 鑿
which collectively are known as his *Sunnah*. Every minute detail of
the Prophet's 鑿 lifestyle, conduct and statements were memorised
by his Companions, who put his example into practice and passed
on reports of what they had seen him do, or had heard from him, to
subsequent generations. These reports or *ahadith* (singular: *hadith*)
were later subjected to intense scrutiny by scholars who recorded
them and classified them into different levels of "soundness" or
authenticity. The greatest recorder of *ahadith* was Imam al-Bukhari,
who spent sixteen years compiling reports of the Prophet's 鑿 words
and deeds in his famous collection of *ahadith, Sahih al-Bukhari*. His
scrupulous attention to detail and authenticity leave us in no doubt
concerning the book he left us.[1]

---

[1]   Imam al-Bukhari was born in 194 AH (c. 800 CE), and from a very early age
demonstrated great zeal, knowledge, and an incredible memory. He travelled
across the newly expanded Islamic state, from Egypt to Persia and from the
Caucasus to the southern tip of Arabia in order to attest to the authenticity of
ahadith. (Continued...)

It is this straightforward presentation, practical application, sincere teaching and equal treatment for all in Islam that have attracted multitudes of people towards the honest teachings of the word of Allah.

The spread of Islam in the Western world has been so rapid that the media has taken to publishing alarmist statistics and issuing "ten–point security plans" to safeguard individuals! The media is at the forefront of creating Islamaphobic environment. The media is unrelenting in it's efforts to misguide people about the truth of Islam, and appears especially keen to convince the world at large that Islam

---

[1] He was so strict in his criteria regarding the *isnad* (chain of narrators) that if he had even a single doubt concerning it, that *hadith* would be omitted from his collection. Imam Abu Hakim states that Imam al-Bukhari laid down the following conditions for including a *hadith* in his *Sahih*: from every Sahabi, at least two Tabi'is should have reported it; and at least two persons who were trustworthy, just and qualified according to the criteria for narrating *ahadith* should have narrated it from each Tabi'i. In this way, the chain of narrators up to Imam al-Bukhari should be unbroken. The Imam interviewed 1080 persons and collected over 300,000 *ahadith*; he himself memorized nearly 200,000, and after applying his stringent criteria, he recorded only 7275 as *sahih* in his book. As a result, there is no doubt about the authenticity of the *ahadith* recorded in *Sahih al-Bukhari*.

Not content with this great achievement, Imam al-Bukhari also compiled an extremely important study on the life of the transmitters of *ahadith*, called *al-Tarikh al-Kabir* (The Great History). Imam al-Bukhari set a precedent for stringent control in recording *ahadith*, so much so that the study of it has become a science in its own right. He always turned to Allah for guidance, and it is reported that no *hadith* was recorded until he had performed ablution and prayed two *rak'ahs* of *salah*. In order to avoid the possibility of social pressures and corruption, Imam al-Bukhari kept away from the company of the Amirs and Sultans of the day. He cared for neither riches nor rich people, and was above flattery and praise. Once the Amir asked him to come to the palace and conduct lessons for him and the princes. The Imam refused, saying, "I do not want to become a flatterer in the royal palace. Such an act will discredit knowledge". The Amir then requested the Imam to appoint a special time in which he would be seen exclusively. Imam al-Bukhari said, "This is the heritage of the Prophet ﷺ. The general people and special people all have equal rights to it. The doors of my seminary and the mosque are open to all and at all times". Such indifference to the powerful and mighty earned him exile from his home town, but for Imam al-Bukhari, Islam came first and he sacrificed everything in order to present a completely accurate report "oppresses" women. But they are failing spectacularly, because – as stated earlier – seven out of every ten Western converts to Islam are women. Within the last decade, an estimated ten thousand British women have accepted and are practising Islam. Most of the new converts are middle class, well-educated, and have professional backgrounds.

Life in Britain today, as in most of the Western world, lacks cohesion, guidance and purpose. "New" Muslims have found the truth and a perfect code of conduct in Islam through which they have improved their life in this world and have definitely secured salvation in the life to come.

In order to fully appreciate the role Islam continues to play in liberating women from cultural oppression which is perpetrated in the name of "freedom", we need to look at women's status through the ages in various societies. I start with an overview of the period prior to the advent of Islam. The second chapter presents the sad and depressing picture of the plight of women who have espoused to the *liasse faire* culture of the Western society. Anyone with the slightest concern for humanity and the social welfare of human beings will be greatly perturbed by some of the calamities faced by women in this supposedly advanced society. I then turn to the teachings of the Qur'an and the Prophet ﷺ on the role, position and integrity of women in Islam.

No book which deals with the issue of women can ignore the aspirations of the feminist movement, so I have included a discussion of their theories. The theories of leading feminists, the views and debates raging within feminism and academia have been reported. I have sought to examine their practical application in the light of Islamic teachings.

I hope and pray that by the time the readers complete the book, they will have gained a deeper insight into the position of women in Islam, the detrimental effect on the moral, social and personal status of the women in the West by adopting and following a way of life suited to their personal desires and finally, a clearer understanding of Islamic teachings on this issue.

   This book is merely an introduction to some of the major topics regarding women. Any shortcomings detected herein are due entirely to my own weaknesses. I pray to Allah for His forgiveness. However, I hope that after reading this work others will be inspired to join in this monumental work of researching and presenting true Islamic teachings, and improve upon my efforts. It is my ardent desire that readers will find the warmth, sincerity and honesty of Islamic teachings reflected in this book, and that this will encourage a deeper understanding of Islam, through which mankind's sufferings and miseries can be elevated.

Ismail Adam Patel
Leicester

Muharram 1418 AH MAY 1997 CE
May 1997

I

WOMAN - A CROSS CULTURE PERSPECTIVE

Islam has achieved far more for women's emancipation and equality than what many of today's feminists realise. Judging Islam by their own secularised and often atheist standards, many members of the feminist's movement denounce the way of life chosen by Allah for woman and man, without knowing or deeply understanding what they are really criticising. It is only Islam that has lifted women from the abyss of oppression to previously unknown levels of freedom and respectability, levels which are unmatched even in today's so-called "civilized" world.

GREEK AND ROMAN CIVILIZATION

In the days of ignorance, prior to the advent of Islam, women in many cultures throughout the world were considered little more than commodities, objects of desire to be bought and sold like livestock. According to Prof. Wil Durant, "In Rome, the man alone had any rights before the law in the early republic; he alone could buy, hold or sell property, or make contracts. Even his wife's dowry in this period belonged to him; if his wife was accused of a crime she was committed to him for judgement, and he could punish her by condemning her to death for infidelity or for stealing the keys to his wine cellar. Over his children he had the power of life, death and sale into slavery... Birth itself was an adventure in Rome. If the child was deformed or female, the father was permitted by custom to expose it to death".[1]

Neither did the Greek philosophers show a great deal of concern for females. Aristotle stated: "... We may thus conclude that it is a natural law that there should be naturally ruling elements and

---

[1] Wil Durant, Caesar and Christ.

---

elements naturally ruled ... The rule of the freeman over the slave is one kind of rule; that of the male over the female another... The slave is entirely without the faculty of deliberation; the female indeed possesses it, but it is a form which remains inconclusive".[1]

The Greeks considered women to belong to the third (lowest) rank of society. If a woman gave birth to a deformed child, it was common practice to kill her. In Sparta, which was acknowledged as an elite society, a woman who could no longer bear children was put to death. The Spartans also took women away from their husbands to be inseminated by "brave and strong men" of other communities. The Greeks in general considered women to be insignificant creatures who could not be dear to the "gods".

Hippolytus' invective against women, in the tragedy by Euripides, sums up the Greek view:

> "O Zeus, whatever possessed you to put an ambiguous misfortune amongst men by bringing women to the light of day? If you really wanted to sow the race of mortals, why did it have to be born of women? How much better it would be if men could buy the seed of sons, paying for it with gold, iron or bronze in your temples, and could live free, without women in their houses".[2]

Judaism

Orthodox Jews who have held on to the classical teachings of Judaism have come under great strain from within as their practices are seen as sexually oppressive. The *Talmud*, a book pertaining to the Jewish civil and ceremonial law, states, 'It is impossible for there to be a world without males and females. Nevertheless happy is the man whose children are males and woe to the man whose children are females'.[3]

---

[1] *Ibid.*

[2] Rubin Suleiman, The Female Body in Western Culture: Contemporary Perspectives, Harvard University Press. 1986.

[3] Alan Unterman, Jews: Their Religious Beliefs and Practices, Routledge & Kegan Paul. London. 1981. Pg 133.

Superiority of the male child is further emphasised by several customs. On the birth of a male child the parents invite guests to a *Kiddush*, a celebratory meal after Sabbath, where there is no such custom after the birth of a female child. In education, it is not considered appropriate to educate the females beyond what is necessary to learn regarding the practices ordained in the Jewish scriptures to the women.[1] When a boy reaches adulthood his maturity is further celebrated by a ritual called, *bar mitzvah*, 'son of the commandment'. The boy who has now become a man can be counted to make up a quorum, *(minyan)*, which is needed for certain prayers and for public worship in the synagogue, for which ten free male adults are required. Whereas women cannot be counted to make up a quorum (*minyan*).[2] There are no parallel celebration for women in Jewish custom. The inequality and injunction towards female oppression is further to be found in the law relating to divorce. A woman has no right of divorce. Even if her husband disappears without trace, without the evidence of his death, she can not remarry[3]. A man has the only right of divorce, and many men have abused this right by abandoning women but not divorcing them, thereby restricting them to remarry.

According to Le Bonn the male Orthodox Jew solemnly recites, "Blessed art Thou, O Lord our God, King of the Universe, that I was not born a female".

The inequalities in Jewish scriptures and traditions is experiencing pressure for change, from within, to be more equitable. The liberating ideologies have brought many changes to Judaism. There has been a recent introduction for the celebration of a girl attaining puberty called *bat mitzvah* (compared with boys called *bar mitzvah*). In education, despite the ruling of Zohar, that the Torah was meant only to be given over to males,[4] the girls education has become an

---

[1]   In the Misnah, a Jewish book of treatise, there is a debate against the prudence of educating women. See also *Ibid.* Pg 140.

[2]   George Foot Moore, Judaism, Cambridge, Harvard Uni. Press. Mass. USA. 1927. Vol 2 Pg 131.

[3]   Leo Trepp, Judaism: Development and Life, Dickenson Pub. Co. Belmont, California. 1966. Pg 191.

[4]   Alan Unterman, *op. cit.* Pg 140.

established feature. In divorce, today the law has been changed so that the couples first turn towards the state courts for seperation and then gain a religious divorce.

HINDUISM

Women fared little better in other belief-systems. In Hinduism, the perfect woman is the *pativrata*, the devoted wife whose entire existence is dedicated to her husband. The very word *pativrata* says it all: "she whose vow (*vrata*) is to her husband (*pati*)". During her lifetime, the good Hindu wife is expected to regard her husband as her own personal god, for the man ordained to be a woman's husband is regarded as far more than a man: he is the incarnation of the supreme law in her life, the definition and summation of her religious duty. After a blameless life, such a woman should ideally die before her husband. If by some mischance she does not, then she may put that right by taking her own life on her husband's funeral pyre. This horrific rite, known as *satee*, was until very recently still being practised in India, and the government has had to intervene to abolish it. Nevertheless, for devout Hindus a woman who is *satee* is worshipped as a goddess, the perfect example of the self-sacrificing wife.[1]

A book on the ancient discipline of Sanskrit religious law, *Draramasastra*, includes a chapter on "the religious status and duties of women," *stridharmapaddhati*. The author (or, more accurately, the compiler) of this work, Tryambaka, was an orthodox pandit living in Thanjavur, in what is now the southern Indian state of Tamil Nadu. The ruling on women generally places them at the level of a subordinate citizen. For example: a wife has no right over her husband's property. Property owned jointly by the wife and husband may be distributed by the husband alone, but the wife needs his permission. Even with various kinds of 'women's property', such as gifts from her husband or her own family, a woman still needs her husband's permission to exercise her rights of ownership.

---

[1]   Archer, Fischle and Wyke, *Women in Ancient Societies*, Macmillan Press. 1994.

Tryambaka's stark message is defined in three ways. Firstly, a wife should have no regard for her own life. Secondly, she should even allow herself to be sold, if her husband should wish it. Thirdly, obedience to her husband takes precedence over all other duties, including religious ones. In essence, however, this law contains only one point: that a woman's highest duty is to her husband.[1]

ARABIA - PRE ISLAM

Prior to Islam, in Arabia, the Arabs treated women with contempt: it was customary for infant girls to be buried alive at birth. Men could have as many wives as they wished, and all were effectively enslaved, and would be inherited as possessions when the husband died. Among the pre-Islamic Arabs, when a man died, his eldest son or other close relative had the right to possess his widow or widows, marrying them himself if he so desired.

Before and during the time of the Prophet Muhammad ﷺ, Persia was ruled by the Sassanids who practised Zoroastrianism. Their faith demanded total obedience of the wife to the husband. A wife was required to declare, "I will never cease, all my life, to obey my husband". Failure to do so would lead to divorce. A wife had no say in any matters and her husband could lend her, for a fee, to others. If a woman did not produce any children, she would be abandoned, if she was lucky; more often than not, a barren wife would be killed.

EUROPE

Britain and most of Europe, in the same period was just recovering from the lengthy Roman occupation, which was followed by the arrival of Christianity. European society was a highly fragmented one, in which tribal wars and kingly struggles to gain control over the land and people were commonplace. With very few exceptions, women had little or no active role to play in such affairs.[2] As the dawn of Islam was starting to illuminate the long shadow of oppression on women, the French in the same period (586 CE) were claiming compassion and civility by passing a resolution, after great

---

[1] *Ibid.*

[2] Erid Delderfield, *Kings and Queens of England and Britain*, David & Charles. 1990.

deliberation and controversy, that woman can be classified as a human being, however she is created for the sole purpose of serving man.[1]

CHRISTIANITY

The title of this section, by definition, is somewhat ambiguous, since the term 'Christianity' covers such a varied set of beliefs and practices. As one commentator put it, "Christianity is always adapting itself into that which is believable". (Or not, as the case may be). The apparent flexibility of this religion creates immediate problems for discussions, since it is easy for anyone to counter what is said about Christianity with the latest amended pronouncements of the Vatican, or Anglican Synod, or of other Churches. It is very much like trying to describe a desert landscape controlled by moving sand. The broad nature of Christian division must also be kept in mind: what holds true in one sect, such as the Church of England (Anglicanism), may not be true in another, such as Roman Catholicism. Nevertheless, if we look to the supposed sources of Christianity, the Old and New Testaments of the Bible, and the scholarly work produced elsewhere, there is sufficient evidence to suggest that women have, over the centuries, received a raw deal from the Mother (!) Church.

According to the Encyclopaedia Britannica, "Christianity did not bring a revolutionary social change to the position of women". Indeed, "in the world of the early church, women were held in very low esteem, and this was the basis for divorce practices that put women practically at men's complete disposal". This is in keeping with the "Old Testament view of marriage as an institution primarily concerned with the establishment of a family, rather than sustaining the individual happiness of the marriage partners", a view which has "strongly influenced" Christianity.

When the "Kingdom of God" is established, marriage which was understood to be a part of the old, passing, order will not exist. According to the Bible as it exists today, the risen ones will "neither marry nor be given in marriage; they will be like the angels in heaven".

---

[1] Maulana Mufti Muhammad Shafi, *Ma'ariful Qur'an*, Maktaba e Darul Uloom Karachi Pakistan. 1996.

(Mark 12:25). Similarly, St. Paul's understanding of marriage in the light of the coming kingdom of God was as follows: "... the time is short. From now on those who have wives should live as if they had none... For the world in its present form is passing away". (1 Corinthians 7:29-30). The early Christians believed that the end of time was relatively near, so marriage was not deemed worthwhile, as it would involve what were regarded as unnecessary troubles: "I would like you to be free from concern" (1 Corinthians 7:32). So it was felt that the unmarried, widowers and widows would fare better if they did not marry. Celibacy was demanded, not only of ascetics and monks, but of increasing numbers of the clergy, as a matter of duty.

The Bible, a book which conclusive evidence proves to have been written by men and to contain only fragments of the original revealed Books given to Prophets over the centuries (including the Torah, Psalms and Gospel), contain many references to the position of women in society. For example:

> "As in all the congregations of the saints, women should remain silent in the churches. They are not allowed to speak, but must be in submission, as the Law says". (1 Corinthians 14:33-34)

The ideology of the female being inferior is indoctrinated from birth:

> "... A woman who becomes pregnant and gives birth to a son will be ceremonially unclean for seven days... If she gives birth to a daughter, for two weeks the woman will be unclean....". (Leviticus 12:1,5)

> "Wives, submit to your husbands... For the husband is the head of the wife as Christ is the head of the Church.....". (Ephesians 5:22-23)

> "Then the Lord God said to the woman, 'What is this you have done?' The woman said, 'The serpent deceived me, and I ate.' ... To the woman he said, 'I will greatly increase your pains in childbearing; with pain will you give birth to children. Your desire will be for your husband, and he will rule over you'." (Genesis 3:13,16)

St. Paul said: "The head of the woman is the man ... for a man ... is the image and glory of God. I suffer not a woman to teach, nor to usurp authority over the man, but to be in silence". [1]

Based on the Biblical image of Eve as a seductive temptress, Christian theologians have historically associated women with sexuality and viewed her with deep suspicion, loathing and fear. Throughout the history of Christianity and the Roman Church, theologians, moralists and ethicists have inveighed against women as corrupt, weak, lustful and evil "daughters of Eve", who are to be shunned and avoided at all costs.[2] The post-Christian feminist Mary Daly insists that since the Genesis stories were written by men, and their conception of God is irrevocably androcentric, they cannot be applied to or by women.[3]

Interestingly, in his 1988 Encyclical, Pope John Paul II stated his belief that mothers are more important than fathers when it comes to raising children. There is no connection between man's procreative role in conception and their social role as fathers, and it is only mothers who are socially defined by their procreative role.[4]

BRITISH HISTORY

English common law stated that upon marriage, a woman lost the rights she possessed when single. All of her property transferred to her husband and both she and it fell under his complete control. He did not even have to account to her. She could not transfer her property, nor enter into contracts in her own name, nor could she sue or be sued. In effect, marriage meant civil death.[5]

A court case in 1840, quoted by O'Faolain and Martines, highlights how insignificantly women were held in British society:[6]

---

[1] Quoted in Julia O'Faolain and Lauro Martines, eds 'Not in God's Image'. New York Harper and Row. 1973

[2] Judith Lorber and Susan Farrell, The Social Construction of Gender, Sage Publications. Newbury Park, California, 1991.

[3] *Ibid.*

[4] *Ibid.*

[5] B S Deckard, *The Women's Movement:* Political, Socioeconomic and Psychological Issues, University of California. 1983.

[6] *Ibid.*

"The question raised in this case is, singularly whether by common law the husband, in order to prevent his wife from eloping, has a right to confine her in his own dwellings and restrain her from liberty, for an indefinite time... There can be no doubt the husband has by law power and dominion over his wife, and may keep her by force... and beat her, but not in a violent or cruel manner".[1]

As late as 1856, women in Britain were not allowed to keep their earnings, and had no rights of inheritance. In that year, women petitioned parliament, which was composed solely of male members, to allow married women to keep their own earnings and inherited property. In 1857, divorced women were granted the same rights as single women, but married women had to wait until 1893 to receive the same rights.

Throughout the nineteenth century, women became more aware of their lack of basic rights in society, and towards the end of the century, a significant movement for change developed, and the suffragettes campaigned for women's right to vote. The political franchise had for centuries been restricted to property-owners only, and had only recently (in the mid-nineteenth century) been extended to all males over the age of 21. Women had to wait until 1928 for this right to be granted to them. Equal pay for equal work took longer: This was not won until 1975. It is clear, then, that Western Europe in general, and Britain in particular, were very late in developing basic rights and equal status for women, contrary to what the moral high ground taken by critics of Islam portray.

This is the global context into which the Prophet of Mercy, Muhammad ﷺ brought his message, and liberated women from the oppression of men and offered them the shade, mercy and equality of Islam. At a time when the entire world treated women with contempt, when women were unable even to question their status, let alone demand basic human and civic rights, Islam came like a beacon blazing forth in the darkness liberating and elevating them.

---

[1] *Ibid.*

To discuss how Islam enhanced the role and status of women in seventh-century Arabia, without addressing present day issues would be a great disservice to the readers. Islam *(submission to the will of the Creator, Allah)* which all the Prophets called to, is the religion for all the people and for all times, equally applicable to all.

How many of today's feminists supposedly, fighting against oppression and subjugation of women, would disagree that women should be viewed as the equals of men? That female infanticide, for any reason, be it social or economic, is evil? That in theological terms, women should be viewed as equal with men in the sight of the Almighty, and be rewarded equally for their virtues? That, as wives, they are entitled to mutual consultation in the affairs of their families? That they should be allowed to possess assets and have a right to their own businesses and incomes? That they should be entitled to inherit from their parents, husbands and other relatives? That they should be allowed to live freely without the fear of being molested or raped? That they should be free from the danger of sexual harassment and should not be portrayed merely as sex-objects or as objects of male desires? That the honour of their bodies be protected from pornographic portrayals? That their suffering in childbirth should be recognised, appreciated and rewarded? For all of these basic rights and more, women of all colours, creeds and social status have had to fight tooth and nail. It is only Islam that has promoted women's rights from the very outset. Islam granted them liberation from the evils of inequality, hundreds of years, before the word "liberation" became fashionable.

II

SOCIAL POSITION OF 'WESTERN WOMEN' TODAY

Now that women conceive to be in charge of their own affairs, does this mean that they have reached the pinnacle of gender equality? Has the "new woman" of today overcome the oppression and subjugation of the "bad old days"? Does the liberation of women signal the advent of a new, morally correct world? Has liberation achieved real emancipation and freed women from injustice? Have we seen the last of oppression, infanticide, prostitution, rape, divorce and single-parent (usually single-mother) families? The answer, according to the feminist should have been an emphatic yes, but is sadly, a dismal no!

The old customs practised by the supposedly "uncivilised" peoples of ancient Rome, Persia, Arabia and Judaea are alive and well but under a new guise. In this modern advanced age, instead of killing innocent girls at birth, we are aborting them in the womb and discarding their mutilated corpses like offal. Abortion is murder, and it has never been heard of a woman's "right to choose" being accepted as defence in a homicide case! Doctors and other abortionists are finding ever more gruesome ways to kill unwanted babies. The latest, which goes by the grotesque name of "partial-birth abortion" involves the partial removal of the foetus from the womb; the head is left inside the mother, and the abortionist (does he or she deserve the title of Doctor?) pierces the back of the skull with a sharp instrument, inserts a catheter, and removes the brains. Then the remains of the murdered child are fully removed. This horrific procedure was devised as a way to get around U.S. laws which state that any child born alive has human rights, and its death would be viewed as murder by the courts. What sort of sick, twisted mind can dream up something like this? Why should a living child in the womb be deserving of fewer rights than one which is already-born?

Women with children are still casually abandoned, as in former centuries. Now the phenomenon is known as "single-parent families". Instead of going to market to purchase a woman, men now resort to prostitution, or even rape. In by-gone times, men murdered women they had no more use for (consider the blood-lust of Henry VIII, founder of the Church of England, and how he disposed of some of his wives); nowadays women are driven towards drugs and alcohol, and ultimately kill themselves. This is labelled as "suicide", and saves men from doing the dirty deed themselves. The old Spartan way of having women "inseminated" by strong men, is now replaced by genetic engineering and artificial insemination via the sperm banks, which achieve the same thing under the auspices of science and technology, the "gods" of their modern age. All of this is regarded as Progress.

Women's equality in the West is a charade. For how long can the world continue to ignore women's misery and the disaster towards which all are heading? The only way to a just, fair and secure future for all is through the pristine teachings of Islam. Muslims have the awesome responsibility of conveying this message correctly and effectively to the people of the world.

According to popular belief, the twentieth century has seen the greatest advancement in equality for women. In particular, the period after the Second World War, from the late 1940s until the present, is hailed as a golden era. But during this period, atrocities of all kinds against women have increased by more than 25%. A survey into the world of government statistics reflect a true picture of the plight of women in today's world.

ABORTION

In Britain, registered abortions have increased almost ten-fold since abortion was "legalised" in 1968. In that year, there were nearly 22,000 registered abortions, compared with nearly 180,000 in 1991. Since records began, there has been a steady increase in the numbers of abortions performed each year. Of the 180,000 abortions that took place in 1991, 110,000 were carried out on unmarried women. Only 1% were done for medical reasons. In 1993, 819,000 women in England and Wales had abortions. The results of population surveys indicate that a third of all conceptions that occurred outside of marriage were terminated by abortion in 1993.[1]

Over 3,000 abortions were carried out on girls aged 15 and under (16 is the "age of consent" in Britain); and over 31,000 termination's were carried out on girls aged 19 and under.

The figures for USA are even more horrific. Abortion rates have increased since records began and there were over one million 'recorded legal abortions' carried out in 1994. The Alan Guttmacher Institute, a research organisation affiliated with Planned Parenthood (America's leading abortion provider – it is rather like calling a butcher a lamb's confidant) estimate the total number of abortions are typically 10 to 20% higher than the official government statistics.[2]

In Canada where the womb is considered to be a safe place for the unborn by the Western standards has nearly half the abortion rate of USA. However, for 1992, this equates to 25% of all pregnancies being terminated by abortion.[3]

In Japan, the 'most advanced' industrial country of the World, where time is money and money is the substance of life, has abortion rates twice that of USA. The nation suffers from over 2 million abortion each year.

The most stupendous blood bath of the innocent unborn life has been carried out in the Former Soviet Union. The Soviet Union suffered an incredible 12.8 million abortions in 1965 out of a total population 233 million. At present almost three quarters of all Soviet women's pregnancies end in abortion.[4]

The trivial nature abortion, human life and women's sentiments are held in the Western world was brought to the forefront when a Charity organisation 'Marie Stopes International' opened six day centres across England. They provided a 'walk-in, walk-out' abortion

---

[1] Home Office, Annual Abstract Statistics, 1996.
[2] National Centre for Health Statistics. Health, *United States*, 1995.
[3] Client Custom Services, *Health Statistics Division* (613-915-1746)
[4] Father Paul Marx, Confessions of a Pro life Missionary. Pub. Human life International, Gaitherburg, Maryland USA. 1988

'that could easily be completed during a working woman's lunch-time break'. Their leading abortionist 'Dr' Tim Black horrified the nation when he disdainfully described the method of abortion by suction as the 'minimal service interception' a 'seamless service without medical drama or moral censure' and a 'quantum leap in service delivery'. Abortion, a traumatic, sorrowful and a grievous moment for every unfortunate woman has been reduced to the language of shopping.[1]

It is worth taking some time to ponder over these figures. Although it is easy to be blinded by such large numbers, we should not forget that each of them is much more than a statistic. Each number represents the murder of an innocent, helpless baby by supposedly "civilized" human beings.

The freedom of choice under the guise of first World civilisation has allowed the hideous slaughter of unborn children which has claimed over ONE BILLION lives throughout the world over the past 25 years.[2]

In the "barbaric" past, infant girls were killed for economic reasons. Now children are killed to destroy the evidence of adultery, fornication and mischief! These figures account only for those abortions which were registered. As for illegal abortions and those carried out in private clinics, only Allah knows exactly how many babies were killed.

RAPE

It is not easy to find accurate figures on rape. Many incidents are not reported, and the police statistics do not include cases where the allegations have been withdrawn. It is safe to assume, therefore, that the official figures are an underestimate.

According to the British police, in 1984 there were over 20,000 cases of indecent assault and nearly 1,500 rape cases in Britain. The London Rape Crisis Centre estimates that there are between 5,000 – 6,000 rapes per year; the true figure may be much higher. Since

---

[1]   Independent On Sunday 29th June 1997.
[2]   The Pro Life Activist Encyclopaedia by the American Life League.

1984, the number of recorded sexual offences has risen at a slightly higher rate than recorded crime in general. By 1994, the number of recorded sexual offences had risen to 32,000.[1] If we accept the higher figures, we may say that, on average, one rape occurs every hour in England. In other words, by the time you finish reading this chapter, someone, somewhere in the country, will have become yet another rape statistic.

The USA, a country proclaiming the greatest freedom of rights has the World's highest rape rate. It is 4 times higher than Germany, 18 times higher than England and almost 20 times higher than Japan. In one state of Utah alone the rape rate is 44.6 per 100,000. In 1995, 2,071 Utah children under the age of 18 were sexually abused: 633 of these children were under the age of 6.[2]

In the USA, 1.3 women are raped every minute. That equates to 78 rapes each hour, 1,872 rapes each day, 683,280 rapes each year.

Looking at such figures, the question springs to mind: who is committing these barbaric acts against women? Are these the acts of mentally disturbed characters roaming the streets? The popular stereotype could not be further from the truth. In 1980, only 2% of men convicted of rape were referred for psychiatric treatment. The reality is shocking and disturbing: over 75% of women who are raped have had some prior contact with the man who raped them.[3] They are raped by acquaintances, people they know and probably trusted. 16% are raped by a close friend or relative.

A study carried out by the National Council for Civil Liberties showed that 38% of men use their power and position at work to rape women. A *Redbook* survey found that 88% of respondents had experienced sexual harassment at work. In the UK, 86% of managers and 66% of employers had experienced such problems. The British Civil Service found that 70% of those surveyed had experienced sexual harassment.[4]

---

1   Criminal Statistics, England & Wales, 1996.
2   Salt Lake Tribune, Sunday, January 12, 1997. Original source - Utah Bureau of Criminal Identification, Crime in Utah, 1995.
3   Rosemarie Tong, Feminist Thought: A Comprehensive Introduction, Routledge.
4   Noami Wolf, *The Beauty Myth*, Vintage.

In Britain, even in that bastion of law and order, the Police service, the problem of sexual harassment is serious. Female officers with twenty-five years' service in the force may be subjected to harassment. Examples of offensive incidents include being spied on while in police stations showers, being "casually" shown pornographic pictures, and being physically groped. One female officer said, "You go into a room and three or four men will run their hands over you to see if you are wearing the 'full tackle,' i.e., suspenders. It happens frequently".[1]

Rape has a devastating emotional, mental and psychological impact on the victims and their families. USA census reports, 1.3 million currently have a mental disorder due to rape, called Rape Related Post Traumatic Disorder (RR-PTSD). 3.8 million in USA have previously had RR-PTSD, and roughly 211,000 women will develop RR-PTSD each year.

MARRIAGE AND DIVORCE

The latter part of the twentieth century has seen an increase in cohabitation i.e., couples "living together" before marriage. Nearly half of women born in the 1960s said that they had cohabited at some time. This social trend is supposed to iron out any difference between partners and ensure that they are compatible before they tie the knot and make the commitment of marriage. This "trial run" is meant to increase the chances of a successful marriage, but the truth is that the increase in cohabitation has been accompanied by an increase in the divorce rate. Britain now has the highest divorce rate in the European Union. In 1983 there were over 147,000 divorces granted by the courts. By 1994, this number had increased to 165,000.[2]

In USA the divorce rate has increased from 708,000 in 1970 to 1,175,000 in 1990. Whereas during the same period the marriage rates have remained virtually static, despite the rise in 'marriageable age' population.[3]

[1]   *The Times*, 7 February 1994.
[2]   Social Trends, 1996.
[3]   US National Centre for Health Statistics 1995

Tables of divorce statistics do not convey the suffering of partners whose marriage breaks down, or of their children whose world is torn apart by the parents' separation. The number of marriages in Britain has decreased, from 389,000 in 1983 to 341,000 in 1994. Of those, nearly one third end in divorce, and the most common grounds for divorce is adultery.

The silent sufferers in divorce families are no doubt the children but even the partners are not saved from the trauma. Divorce now ranks as the number one factor linked with suicide rates in USA, outstripping other important social and economic predictors. Divorced people are three times more likely to commit suicide than people who are married.[1]

The more human beings rely on their own intellectual reasoning and abandon the guidance of their Creator, the greater their suffering.

SINGLE PARENTS

There is yet another set of depressing statistics that has been increasing since the advent of so-called "women's liberation". In the past ten years, the number of births to unmarried mothers has risen from nearly 90,000 in 1982 to 215,000 in 1992. Of all the babies born in 1992, 31% were born to unwed mothers. Nearly 2,500 girls under the age of 15 gave birth, and over 23,000 new mothers in that year were aged under 20.[2]

As the number of illegitimate births has increased , the number of babies born within marriage has decreased, from 890,000 in 1961 to 511,000 in 1994. The reality behind these statistics is that women are bearing most, if not all, of the responsibility for raising these children. This form of oppression of women should not be ignored; men must be made to shoulder the responsibility and be accountable for the children they produce.

An official survey has demonstrated that the number of families with children headed by a lone parent has risen to more than one in five (over 20%); in the North West of England, the figure is closer to

---

[1]   The Detroit News, September 1, 1995
[2]   *Ibid.*

30%, or one in three. The same survey shows that fewer than 60% of women aged 18-49 are married. Even more alarmingly, growing numbers of single mothers are typically trying to cope on very little money: 42% of them had a gross weekly income of less than £100.[1] The impact of poverty on educational achievement, crime rates, health, moral value and self esteem has been well-documented and has led to reports in Britain and elsewhere of an "emerging underclass" whose future is indescribably bleak.

The burden of family care on the Western women has been escalating and in 1994, the USA had 9.9 million single mothers having to maintain and take care of their children compared with only 1.6 million single fathers. The 'normal house' with a father, mother and children has become an illusion in the Western world and is reaping havoc. The USA – In 1970, 40% of household were made up of married couples. In 1995, only 25% of households are made up of married couples.[2] The social impact of single parenting on children is devastating. 75% of children in chemical dependency hospitals are from single parent families.[3] 20% of children in single parent families have a learning, emotional or behavioural problem.[4] 63% of suicides are committed by individuals from single parent families.[5]

The burden on woman created by 'single parenting' is one of the most brutal forms of oppression.

HEALTH

When it comes to health matters, women fare less well than men, especially when it comes to mental health. Single mothers, in particular, suffer poorer health than women in two-parent households. General Health Survey data indicate that lone mothers are more likely to have both long-standing and recent illness, and

1   Kimball Young, Isn't One Wife Enough? Henry Holt and Co. New York. 1954.
2   US Census Bureau 'Household and Family Characteristics' : March 1995.
3   Centre for Disease Control, Atlanta.
4   National Centre for Health Statistics.
5   FBI Law Enforcement Bulletin.

are less likely to assess their health over the last twelve months as good. In this survey, only 43% of single mothers described their health as "good" and nearly 39% reported a long-standing illness.[1]

Women also suffer poorer psychological health than men. They see their GPs (family doctors) more often for mental health problems, and are more frequently prescribed drugs for anxiety and depression.[2] Women are more unwell and unhappy than men because of the work they do and the conditions in which they do it[3] created by the capitalist system for the acquiring of profit margins.

If you were to question a randomly-picked sample of the population and ask them, "Who suffers more from mentally-related disorders?" The majority will reply: women. However, this has not always been the case. Studies from 1850 until the Second World War show that men used to be more prone to mental disorders than women. In the majority of studies prior to 1950 or the Second World War, the overall rates were higher for men.[4]

In the case of women's mental health, the findings differ sharply from the 1950s onwards, with the advent of so-called equal status. A report by B P Dohrenwend in the *American Journal of Sociology* shows that while prior to 1950, for every 7 men diagnosed as mentally ill, only 2 women were similarly diagnosed, after 1950, the ratio changed to 22 women for every 2 men. This catastrophic reversal in mental illness statistics accompanied the rise of "women's liberation" in the West.

This increased incidence of mental illness among Western women since the Second World War has occurred because "... women find their position in society to be more frustrating and less rewarding than do men ..".[5] The reason for this greater sense of frustration may be found in the unfair burden which is placed on the "liberated"

---

[1]   Hilary Graham, *Hardship and Health in Women's Lives*, Harvester Wheatsheaf. New York. 1993.
[2]   Office of Population survey, 1993.
[3]   Hilary Graham, *op. cit.*
[4]   Gove & Tudor, *Adult Sex Roles and Mental Illness.*
[5]   *Ibid.*

women. She is expected to display masculine traits in the workplace, but is also supposed to maintain her "femininity" – a dual burden that is too heavy for many women, who may eventually break down.

Mental illness researchers have also discovered that single persons are more prone to mental illness than those who are married, and their prognosis is not as good. As early as the turn of the century, Durkheim noted that the severing of the marital tie is particularly dangerous for mental health, as indicated by a high suicide rate among the widowed and divorced. Since that time, all studies[1] comparing the mental health of those who are widowed or divorced with that of those who are married have also found that the rates of mental illness are higher among the former. With the rise of the divorce rate, the prospect of women's mental health looks particularly poor.

ALCOHOL AND SMOKING

The Western development of the equality of the sexes has been accompanied by an increase in the vices that were previously thought to be a male preserve, namely the consumption of alcohol and tobacco. According to a recent report published in the Sunday Times, the number of women drinking more than the "recommended limit" is rising. The survey shows that the number of men exceeding this limit has fallen to 26%, whilst the number of women doing so has risen to 12%.

Smoking used to be a men's vice, as for a long time it was deemed improper for women to smoke. However, the number of women who smoke is now more or less the same as the number of men who do so. Although anti-smoking campaigns have led to many adults quitting the habit, tobacco companies have responded by targeting younger people, on the premise that if they can get teenagers or children "hooked" they will continue to have a ready market for their product. Reports indicate that more young women than young men are starting to smoke, which indicates that in the near future the majority of smokers will be women.

---

[1]   Hugh Freeman, Progress in Mental Health, Churchill, London. 1958.

PORNOGRAPHY

The rapid growth of the pornographic industry since the 1950s has, again, mirrored the progress of "equality" in the West. Pornography does not present women as human beings with feelings and needs, but as mere available commodities to be used and cast aside. Women are led to believe that by selling their bodies, they are achieving equality, but in fact they become subordinate to men who use the idea of equality to exploit women for their own desires and financial gain.

In the 1980s, a further step in the manipulation of women appeared. Sheila Jeffreys, a feminist, wrote: "When the campaign against pornography first got underway, it was possible to attack pornography as a male product designed for male consumption. This is not true in the 1980s. Women are being told – by libertarian theorists - that because 'women are equal now,' it is all right for women to enjoy pornography. This ideology serves more to defeat women's emancipation than to pander to it. The idea of selling pornography to women from the 1980s has become a more sophisticated and effective way of bolstering male power".

Pornography is the biggest media category world-wide. It enters our homes via television and magazines, as well as video, film and satellite media. Globally, pornography generates $7 billion annually, more than the legitimate film and music industries combined. In the US, pornographic films gross $1 million daily, and outnumber films of other genres by 30%. In Britain, 20 million copies of pornographic magazines are sold each year, producing an annual revenue of over £500 million. In Sweden, a large "sex shop" may offer over 500 titles of pornographic magazines, and a corner shop can offer up to 50 titles. It is estimated that 18 million American men buy a pornographic magazine each month.[1] Pornography throughout the world is becoming ever more violent and gruesome, and is spreading further via the new technology: pornography on the Internet, including "hard-core" and child pornography, is a growing problem worldwide. The Western world is also exporting this deviant trend, which exploits women in the most abhorrent fashion, to the so-called third world.

---

[1]   Naomi Wolf, *op. cit.*

This is the state of affairs to which Western "civilization" and its "progress" and "equality" have brought humankind, where women are victimised in ever increasing numbers to vices and mistreatment that any sane person would abhor and seek to eliminate.

To summarise, within the last hour the following have taken place in England: one woman was raped, eighteen people got divorced, 20 women had abortions, and 24 children were born to women without husbands. These same events will be repeated in the next hour, and in the hour after that. As you go through your daily routine of sleeping and waking, this sorry state of events will continue, and the number of victims will continue to escalate.

What possible answer can there be? How can these barbaric crimes against women be reduced, if not eliminated altogether? The path of supposed equality between the sexes is only making the problem worse, and any sane person can see that the world is moving away from a civilized state towards a position of barbarity and ignorance (*jahiliyyah*). Very much like that which prevailed before the advent of Islam. In a society which considers itself to be at the forefront of civility and human concerns, how can the low standards of morality that prevail nowadays be accepted?

What are the solutions to these problems? For the people who are blessed with sincerity and understanding, there is no need to search far afield. Who better to guide, than the Creator of men and women, Allah Himself? When comparing Western practices to the values of Islam, it will soon be apparent where people have gone wrong and how Islam may steer people back on to the right path.

The single most common cause of the problems discussed above is the fact that Western society encourages the free mixing of men and women. The natural modesty of one sex towards the other is regarded as backward, unfashionable and uncivilized. Any effort to retain a sense of modesty is immediately labelled as "oppressive" or "repressive". Yet considering the disastrous consequences of free mixing, from the above statistics, the appropriate course of behaviour to be undertaken is clear.

Recent Psychologists reports[1] agree that when there are two persons of opposite genders in enclosed surroundings, sexual ideas and connotations are bound to pass through their minds. The casual and frequent manner in which such encounters are allowed to occur in an atmosphere of free mixing sets the stage for most of the calamities suffered by women today. Acting upon these impulses leads to all the woes of modern society: Abortion, divorce, single parent families, suicide, rape and all the other heart-breaking social ills. Fourteen hundred years ago, the Prophet Muhammad ﷺ warned humanity about the hazards of free mixing and advised extreme caution. In this matter, he informed us that *when a man and a woman are alone together, the third one present will be the Shaytan (Satan)*[2], working to implant mischief between the two.

As stated earlier, 75% of all rapes are committed by men who know their victims personally. In the workplace, 38% of men in positions of power abuse their position to take advantage of women working with them. The most frequent cause of divorce is adultery, which is made easy by the free mixing of the sexes. The reason that children as young as 15 are getting pregnant is because the schools, which were once segregated, have become "co-educational", and are now dens of iniquity where peer pressure reigns supreme and promiscuity is the order of the day. The abortion rate simply reflects the low esteem in which human life is held.

In the Western world, equality for women has meant looking the same as men, doing the same jobs as them, and exhibiting the same behaviour and characteristics as men. Western societies have paid the price for this unnatural approach, by suffering huge losses of morality and human values. Equality of the sexes does not mean that both men and women should look the same. In a society where money, beauty and masculinity are what counts, a woman has to work, dress and behave like a man and at the same time stay pretty like a model in order to stand on equal terms with men. This is to the detriment of her moral values and feminine nature.

---

[1]   Time Magazine - June 1, 1997.
[2]   Abu Dawood. Sunan al Tirmidhi trans. Prof. Ahmad Hasan. Pub.Sh Muhammad Asraf, Lahore, Pakistan.

Islam has set out the unique and complementary roles of both men and women, an issue which will be examined more closely later. First, the misinformation campaign directed at most Westerners which conveys to them that Islam preaches inhuman practices and the oppression of women need to be emphasised. Opponents of Islam usually maliciously manipulate the fact that Muslim women are required to dress modestly, and are prohibited from mixing freely with the opposite sex. A further whip is drawn to bash Islam with by distorting the facts regarding polygny. They misconstrue these Islamic teachings as evidence and portray Islam as preaching suppression of women. The West has been so successful in propagating these distorted views that even some Muslims have fallen victim to it. This should hardly come as a surprise when it is known that Muslims tend to be more familiar with Western literature than their own Islamic heritage. In Britain alone, between 1960 and 1978 over 22,000 books and 43,000 journals published material slandering the teachings of Islam. When every form of media and education such as, television, schools, teachers, friends, colleagues, books, newspapers and magazines are all conveying this distorted message that Islam oppresses women; it is no wonder that those who are poorly educated, in the facts of the matter, are so easily distracted away from the right path.

To counter this tide of misinformation, a general need to educate society at large about the true Islamic teachings regarding women needs to be urgently undertaken. The Qur'an and *ahadith* are quite explicit on this matter and the next chapter explains the proper status of women in Islam according to these sources.

III

WOMEN IN ISLAM

SPIRITUAL EQUALITY OF THE SEXES

In many other religions, women have had to fight for their rights and dues, and their struggle, in many cases, is still ongoing. Christian women, for example, have had to struggle to make their voices heard, and have gone to the extreme of changing the text of the Bible to make it less "sexist" and more "acceptable" to women. Islam, on the other hand, has justly granted women their rights without them having to ask, let alone demand and fight.

> For Muslim men and women - for believing men and women, for devout men and women, for true men and women, for men and women who are patient and constant, for men and women who humble themselves, for men and women who give in charity, for men and women who fast (and deny themselves), for men and women who guard their chastity, and for men and women who engage much in Allah's praise - for them has Allah prepared forgiveness and great reward.
>
> *[al-Ahzab 33:35]*

A number of Islamic virtues are mentioned here, but the primary message of this *ayah* is that these virtues are applicable to both, women as well as men. Both sexes have human rights and duties to an equal degree, and the rewards of the Hereafter are available to men and women alike.[1] Each individual will be judged according to his or her deeds. Gender is simply not an issue in this matter.

> And their Lord has accepted of them, and answered them: 'Never shall I suffer to be lost the

work of any of you, be he male or female: you are
members, one of another...

[Al 'Imran 3:195]

Allah has granted the prayers of the Believers, and has told us that
He will not let the labour of any individual go to waste. Everyone
will reap the reward of his or her efforts. A woman may achieve this
just as a man may. Man and woman alike are members of the human
race, created from the same source and joined by Islam as partners
in life and in reward.[1]

> Whoever works righteousness, man or woman,
> and has Faith, verily, to him will We give a new
> Life, and life that is good and pure, and We will
> bestow on such their reward according to the best
> of their action.
>
> *[al-Nahl 16: 97]*

The spiritual equality of women to men in Islam is abundantly
clear, so nobody should fall for the prejudiced view propagated by
the Islamaphobes in the Western media.

From the time a child is conceived, Islam gives glad tidings to a
woman regardless of the gender of the foetus. The pregnant woman
is held in the highest esteem, and her patience in bearing the
discomforts of pregnancy is regarded as an act of virtue which brings
her closer to Paradise. If the baby is a girl, this opens up further
opportunities for the parents to attain Paradise. In stark contrast to
the attitude of the pagan Arabian society which buried female babies
alive (and the modern *jahiliyyah* in which many societies views the
birth of a girl as bad news), the Prophet ﷺ gave the glad tidings of
Paradise as the reward for the one who welcomes a daughter, brings
her up properly, provides a sound education and arranges a good
marriage for her.[1] In another *hadith*, it is stated that the fire of Hell
will not be permitted to touch one who goes through trials and

---

[1]   Yusuf Ali, note 3619 - The Holy Quran, trans. Yusuf Ali, Pub. Islamic
      Propogation Centre International, Medina. 1946.
[2]   Allama Shabbir Ahmed Usmani, *The Holy Qur'an*, English trans. Mohammad
      Ashfaq Ahmed, Idara Isha'at-E-Diniyat, Lucknow India. 1992.

tribulations because of a daughter, but still does not hate her, and treats her well.[2]

The Qur'an expressively forbids killing babies, whether by infanticide or abortion, for fear of poverty or losing face in the community:

> Say: 'Come, I will rehearse what Allah has (really) prohibited you from: join not anything as equal with Him; be good to your parents; kill not your children on a plea of want - We provide sustenance for you and for them – come not nigh to shameful deeds, whether open or secret; take not life, which Allah has made sacred, except by way of justice and law: thus does He command you, that you may learn wisdom.
>
> *[al-An'am 6:151]*

The Qur'an also tells us that the innocent girls who were slain for no other reason than that they were female, will be asked on the Day of Judgement for what sin they were slain:

> When the female (infant) buried alive, is questioned – for what crime she was killed
>
> *[al-Takwir 81:8-9]*

The crime is that of the parents, not of the child. Parents should not think that they are at liberty to do whatever they like with regard to their children. It is almost beyond belief that in the modern world the practice of infanticide, in the epithet of abortion, can be allowed to exist. China is currently experiencing an epidemic of this barbarism, under its strict population control laws; families are allowed only one child, and most parents want sons, so girls are abandoned and allowed to die, or are killed, so that the parents may have another child, hopefully a boy. The Western nations, which are so quick to condemn China, are not so far behind in savagery, except they have sanitised infanticide in the guise of abortion.

---

1   Imam al-Bukhari, *Sahih al-Bukhari*, trans. Muhammad Muhsin Khan, Islamic University, Al Medina al Munawara. Pub. Lahore Pakistan, Kazi Publications. 1984.

Not only does the Qur'an protect the female infant from being murdered by ignorant parents, but it describes her birth as good news, and grants her the right of inheritance from her father, husband and brother, and gives her the right to own property and conduct business transactions independently and in her own right.

> When news is brought to one of them, of (the birth of) a female (child), his face darkens and he is filled with inward grief! With shame does he hide himself from his people, because of the news that he has had! Shall he retain it on (sufferance and) contempt, or bury it in the dust? Ah! What an evil (choice) they decide on.
>
> *[al-Nahl 16:58-59]*

This *ayah* refers to the period of *Jahiliyyah*, just before the advent of Islam, when it was the custom of the pagan Arabs to bury female infants alive. Islam totally forbids such crimes, but sadly this evil practice is still continuing in many communities, where women are not valued and are seen as a burden. At the very least, the birth of a girl is resented and she may be neglected whilst the best food and education is given to her brothers; at the worst, modern technology is exploited so that if a female foetus is detected via an ultrasound scan, it may be aborted, whilst a male foetus will be carried to full term.

The spiritual equality of the sexes in Islam extends to the worldly plane, and education is required both for male and female. The Prophet ﷺ said: "Seeking knowledge is a duty for every Muslim male and female". He also urged Muslims to "Seek knowledge from the cradle to the grave".

The importance of seeking knowledge cannot be over-emphasised. All Muslims are urged to educate themselves, to act upon their knowledge, and to convey it to others.

> ... Those truly fear Allah, among His Servants, who have knowledge.
>
> *[Fatir 35:28]*

It is only those with knowledge and understanding who will be truly conscious of the glory and transcendency of Allah. They will understand the transience of the present world and the permanence of the Hereafter, and thus they will be concerned about their future and will strive to attain knowledge of the Divine guidance.

Islam promotes the education of both sexes. Islamic history, from the very beginning, records the names of numerous female scholars, foremost among whom is 'A'ishah ﷺ[1], who was one of the greatest narrators of *ahadith*. Not only was she responsible for conveying over two thousand *ahadith*, but the great men of her time used to consult with her on matters of *fiqh (jurisprudence)*.

MARRIAGE

There is no celibacy in Islam. Islam considers sexuality to be a natural part of life, which is to be channelled into a healthy marriage life; sinful fulfilment of the sexual urge and exploitation of women through prostitution, pornography and rape are utterly forbidden.

The Prophet ﷺ advised Muslims: "Whoever is able to marry, should marry, for that will help him lower his gaze and guard his modesty".[2] As well as providing a legitimate channel for sexual energy - which will keep a person away from sin – marriage provides comfort, security, solace and companionship. Islam not only regards marriage as necessary, but has raised it to the level of being a positive virtue, whereby those who marry will be rewarded for doing so, as for any other good deed. The Prophet ﷺ emphasised the importance of marriage when he described it as being half of faith.[3]

An important condition of marriage is that this union should be by the consent of both partners; neither male nor female should be forced into a marriage. In particular – as a warning against the oppression of women – Islam clearly states that a marriage contracted without the free consent of the woman is null and void. The Prophet ﷺ said: "No widow should be married without consulting her, and

---

[1] May Allah be pleased with her.
[2] *Sahih al Buhkari op. cit.*
[3] *Ibid.*

no virgin should be married without her consent..".[1]

Prospective marriage partners are encouraged to see one another before they agree to marry. Jabir ﵁[2] reported that the Messenger of Allah ﷺ said, "When one of you seeks to marry a woman, if he is able to have a look at the one he desires to marry, let him do so".[3]

Above all, marriage in Islam is a contract between two equal parties. As an equal partner, the Muslim woman may stipulate conditions in the marriage. In contrast to British women, who even now do not have the right to draw up a contract or stipulate conditions, Muslim women were given this right fourteen hundred years ago. The woman may stipulate, prior to marriage, conditions, including the transfer of divorce power to herself, restricting the husband to one wife only, and clearly defining the conditions of maintenance.[4]

Marriage in Islam is much more than a means of satisfying sexual desires; it is a social contract of co-habitation through which both partners may find companionship and a refuge from the trials and tribulations of life. In Islam, a woman is not seen as an object for male gratification or a workhorse who is expected to cater to every need and whim of the male. She is a spiritual and moral being who is brought into union with a man on the basis of a solemn pledge which Allah is called upon to witness. The Prophet ﷺ is reported to have said, "You have seen nothing like marriage for increasing the love of two people".[5]

Today in the West, married women who retain their maiden names are viewed as feminists or unusually self-assertive. Muslim women, however, have always been allowed and expected to keep their maiden names after marriage. This right to maintain their own identity was given to women in Islam when elsewhere in the world

---

[1] Imam Muslim, *Sahih Muslim*, trans. Abdul Hamid Siddiqi, Kitab Bhavan, India. 1979.

[2] May Allah be pleased with him

[3] Abu Dawud, trans. Prof. Ahmad Hasan, Pub. SH. Muhammad Ashraf, Lahore Pakistan. 1984.

[4] Maulana Zahier Ragie, *Kitabun Nikah*, Madrasa Arabia Islamia, South Africa. 1992.

[5] *Mishkat* al Masabih, trans. James Robson, Pub SH Muhammad Ashraf, Lahore Pakistan. 1994.

women were seen as being barely human and debates raged as to whether they even possessed a soul, let alone be given independence.

The Qur'an describes marriage in the most moving and eloquent terms:

> ... They [wives] are your garments and you [husbands] are their garments....
>
> *[al-Baqarah 2:187]*

> And among His Signs is this, that He created for you mates from among yourselves, that you may dwell in tranquillity with them, and He has put love and mercy between your (hearts): verily in that are Signs for those who reflect.
>
> *[al-Rum 30:21]*

> It is He Who created you from a single person, and made his mate of like nature, in order that he might dwell with her (in love)..
>
> *[al-A'raf 7:189]*

> (He is) the Creator of the heavens and the earth: He has made for you pairs from among yourselves..
>
> *[al-Shura 42:11]*

In Islam, there is no notion of woman being responsible for the "Fall" or of being the first sinner and therefore responsible for all of the mankind's woes. There is no idea of man being created out of superior material and woman out of base matter. Woman is made equal, both men and women are the progeny of Adam, so both have similar souls.[1]

> mankind! Reverence your Guardian – Lord Who created you from a single Person, created, of like nature, his mate, and from them twain scattered (like seeds) countless men and women – fear Allah, through Whom you demand your mutual (rights).
>
> *[al-Nisa' 4:1]*

---

[1]   Abdul Wahid Hamid, *Islam, the Natural Way*, MELS, London. 1989

> And Allah has made for you mates (and
> companions) of your own nature, and made for
> you, out of them, sons and daughters and
> grandchildren. And provided for you sustenance
> of the best: will they then believe in vain things,
> and be ungrateful for Allah's favours?
>
> *[al-Nahl 16:72]*

Islam does not view woman as the instrument of the devil, as is asserted by Christian teachings. The Qur'an describes woman as *muhsanah*, a fortress against evil, because a good woman helps her husband maintain the path of righteousness.[1]

Muslim men are continually admonished to treat their wives kindly. To those men who oppress their wives:

> O you who believe! You are forbidden to inherit
> women against their will. Nor should you treat
> them with harshness, that you may take away part
> of the dower you have given them - except when
> they have been guilty of open lewdness; on the
> contrary live with them on a footing of kindness
> and equity. If you take a dislike to them it may be
> that you dislike a thing, and Allah brings about
> through it a great deal of good.
>
> *[al-Nisa' 4:19]*

Men are commanded by Allah to consort with women amicably and honourably. They should refrain from harshness in speaking to and dealing with them. Behaviour that goes against standards of morality and common courtesy is prohibited. Such wicked and brutal conduct is the sign of ignorance (*jahiliyyah*) which Islam came to abolish.[2]

Muslims are admonished to treat women equitably. The Qur'an forbids them to inherit women and abuse them, sexually or otherwise, as was the custom prior to the advent of Islam and as is still practised

---

[1] *Ibid.*
[2] Usmani, *op. cit.*

in many societies where the rich and strong take advantage of the poor and weak in this way. This Islāmic rule applies not only to the Arabs of the seventh century CE, but to all subsequent generations of Islam. Men are forbidden to abuse women, and are commanded to live amicably with their marriage-partners. The command of Allah to do so is reinforced by the comment that while a man may find some trait or aspect of his wife's behaviour that he dislikes, it may be that Allah will bring about something good if he tolerates it graciously and accepts his wife for what she is. In all of this there is benefit for the man.

The Prophet ﷺ enhanced this message of equality and fair treatment of women by setting the supreme example for mankind to observe and emulate. He demonstrated the importance of taking care of oneself and one's daily needs, instead of imposing on one's wife. Accounts of his life give numerous examples which "modern men" may learn from. He ﷺ attended to his own personal needs, he helped his wives in the house, and he even stitched and mended his own clothes. He ﷺ demonstrated that a man is never too great to clean and look after himself, and he imparted the following advice:

> "The best among you is the one who is best to his family, and I am the best among you to his family".[1]

> "The most perfect believers are the best in conduct and the best of you are those who are best to their wives".[2]

> "Many women have come to the family of Muhammad complaining about their husbands... Those husbands are not the best of you".[3]

> "By assisting your wives in their household duties, you will receive the reward of sadaqah (charity)".[4]

[1]   Mishkat al-Masabih, op.cit.
[2]   Imam Tirmidhi, Sunan al Timidhi, Karachi Pakistan, Idara Ishat. 1985.
[3]   Riyadh al Salihin, trans. S.M. Madni Abbasi, International Islamic Pub. Lahore, Pakistan. 1991.
[4]   *Ibid*

"A believer must not hate a believing woman; if he dislikes one of her characteristics, he should be pleased with another".[1]

"When a woman breast feeds, for every gulp of milk she will receive a reward as if she had granted life to being, and when she weans her child, the angels pat her on the back saying, 'Congratulations! All your past sins have been forgiven, now start all over again".[2]

"O women! Remember that the pious among you will enter Jannah before the pious men".[3]

"During pregnancy until the time of childbirth, and until the end of the suckling period, a woman earns reward similar to that of the person who is guarding the borders of Islam".[4]

In his famous speech given during his Farewell Pilgrimage, in which he ﷺ reiterated the most important points of Islamic teaching, the Prophet ﷺ reminded the Muslims of the importance of treating women equitably: "O people, fear Allah with regard to women..". Once again, men are reminded to remember Allah and fear His retribution, for Allah is aware of everything that passes between them.

'A'ishah ؆ reported that when the Prophet ﷺ was home, he would help with the household chores, treat his family amicably, and maintain a pleasant atmosphere in the home.

Islamic teachings are very strict when it comes to the fair treatment of others, and in the case of physical superiority Islam clearly states the responsibilities of the stronger party. As women are physically weaker, they are entitled to protection, and men are answerable for any misuse of their physical strength against women. All kinds of physical abuse are forbidden in Islam, which also prohibits

[1] *Ibid.*
[2] *Ibid.*
[3] Beheshti Zewar, Maulana Ashraf Ali Thanwi, Dini Book Depot, New Delhi
[4] Al-Tabarani.

41

psychological abuse such as seclusion and unnecessary restriction of movement and travel. A husband is also forbidden to disclose his wife's secrets, as the Prophet ﷺ said: "the worst of all people is the one who approaches his wife, enjoys her company, then divulges her secrets".[1]

Marriage is in accordance with the teachings of Islam, so whatever permissible deeds are done within the context of marriage - including sex - are regarded as virtues. The Prophet ﷺ once said, "A man will be rewarded for his physical relations with his wife". His listeners, somewhat surprised, asked, "Will a person be rewarded for satisfying his passions?" The Prophet ﷺ replied, "Do you not see that if he were to satisfy his passions in a forbidden manner he would be committing a sin? So if he satisfies himself in a lawful manner, he will be rewarded".[2]

The importance of the physical side of marriage is also referred to in a *hadith* narrated by Imam al-Bukhari. The Prophet ﷺ is reported to have upbraided one of his Companions, who was going to extremes in his devotion to worship: "O Abdullah, have I not been informed that you fast all day and stand in prayer all night?" Abdullah said, "Yes, O Messenger of Allah". He said, "Do not do that. Observe the fast at some times and refrain from fasting at others. Stand in prayer at night, then sleep. Your body has a right over you, your eyes have a right over you and your wife has a right over you".

Islam regards men and women as equal partners who should co-operate in making the home, community and society at large harmonious, happy and successful. The partners should be loyal, considerate and dependent upon one another. They should work together to overcome any problems and obstacles. They should be jointly concerned with their children's upbringing and education, and work together to meet their children's needs. They should work together to overcome the shortcomings of each partner, and present a united front to the outside world. They should also provide companionship and comfort to one another.

[1]   Imam Muslim, *op. cit.*
[2]   *Ibid.*

Certain Qur'anic references have given rise to much debate concerning women's role, rights and duties.

> ... And women shall have rights similar to the rights against them, according to what is equitable; but men have a degree (of advantage) over them.
>
> *[al-Baqarah 2:228]*

There are various points of view as to the significance of the phrase "a degree (of advantage)". Some suggest that it means the qualities of leadership, surveillance and maintenance that are given to men. Others favour the idea that it refers to the tolerance which is expected of men even when their wives are in an extremely bad mood. Another opinion is that it is man's natural gift, bestowed by Allah, for judging family matters and managing problems that may arise. However, the consensus of most scholars is that, this "degree" refers to the principle of guardianship, and nothing more.[1] In another *ayah*, the Qur'an says:

> Men are the protectors and maintainers of women, because Allah has given the one more (strength) than the other, and because they support them from their means...
>
> *[al-Nisa' 4:34]*

Commenting on this verse, Yusuf Ali states that the difference in economic position between the sexes makes the man's rights and liabilities a little greater than the woman's. This verse refers to the duty of the man to maintain the woman, and to a certain difference in the nature of the two genders. However, the two sexes are seen as being on equal terms in law, and in certain matters the "weaker sex" (the female) is entitled to special protection.[2] It should be borne in mind that the Qur'an offers guidance for all human societies at all periods of history. So Islam seeks to maximise the benefit of all women, worldwide.

---

[1] Maulana Mufti Ahmed Bemat, *The Muslim Woman*, Madani Kutubkhana.
[2] Yusuf Ali, *The Holy Qur'an*, op.cit.

Abdullah ibn Abbas ❁, a companion of the Prophet ❁, mentioned, with reference to the *ayah* quoted above, that as men have been granted such a noble position by Allah, they should exercise greater patience. If there is some deficiency on a wife's part, then the husband's position demands that he should accommodate her weaknesses, maintain a patient attitude, and establish consistency in the fulfilment of his rights. In short, marriage is intended to bring mutual benefits to both partners.

A renowned Asian scholar, Hazrat Hakim Akhtar saheb states: "the rights of women have been mentioned before those of men in this verse because man, due to his inherent power and strength, easily obtains his rights from the woman. Thus Allah placed more emphasis upon the rights of women who cannot forcibly obtain their rights".[1] The second point that may be noted from this *ayah* is that the man should take the initiative in fulfilling his responsibilities, because the Qur'an has mentioned women's rights first.

The "degree above" cannot, and must not, be taken to imply male superiority of worth. What it does imply is a greater liability and responsibility, which means that men will be subjected to greater questioning in the Hereafter regarding the treatment of their wives and families. This is hardly what could be described as an enviable position, and some may even consider it "inferior"! The degree in question is nothing more than a means of assuring the maintenance of women, as and when it is necessary.

Islam clearly recognises the equal potential and ability of the sexes, but Allah has created human beings in a manner whereby men and women are better suited for differing but complementary, tasks. Just because the male may be better at a given task than the female, it does not mean that he is inherently superior. This is an error made by many feminists, who assume that liberation may be achieved by adopting a male role. Instead of recognising and cherishing their femininity, they seek to ape men, to the detriment of women and human society in general. By aspiring to male traits, values and behaviour, they have further diminished the female whilst elevating

---

[1]   Mufti Zubair Bayat, *The Status of Women in Islam*, Jet Printers, South Africa.

the male. By equating financial earnings and following a career with prestige and status, the feminine pursuits of motherhood, household work and the raising of a family have become valueless and are seen as degrading. Because unpaid work is seen as worthless, household work is viewed as demeaning drudgery. In contrast, Islam emphasises harmony and mutual dependency, so a woman's work in caring for the home and raising the family is seen as being as essential and important as a man's work in earning money for the financial support of the family.

Mankind has been infected with the capitalist bug, where any type of work not providing a financial income is considered oppressive. The simple truths, taught by Islam, have become too difficult to accept. Humanity should not allow itself to be dazzled by the West and fooled into denigrating women's valuable work. In Islam, the woman's role is very important, perhaps even more important than that of a man. As we have seen, the acts of childbearing and suckling – roles which are open only to women – bring immense rewards. Although these abilities are a gift granted by the Creator, the woman exercises an element of choice whether to breast feed as a means of earning this reward. Moreover, as her share of the childrearing burden is greater, from the moment of conception onwards, Allah the All-Merciful and All-Wise has made the woman a means by which any individual may attain Paradise, in that Paradise is described as lying at the feet of mothers (see also the *ahadith* on the virtues of mothers, below). The hardships and tribulations suffered by women during pregnancy, birth, suckling and childrearing, are not wasted. They bring the promise of compensation, reward and a higher status in this world and the next.

MOTHERHOOD

The Prophet ﷺ indicated that a woman's status is further enhanced when she becomes a mother. A man once asked him ﷺ, "Who deserves the best care from me?" He ﷺ replied, "Your mother". The man asked, "Then who?" He ﷺ replied, "Your mother". The man asked, "Then who?" He ﷺ replied, "Your mother". The man asked, "Then who?" He ﷺ replied, "Then your father".[1]

---

[1] *Imam al-Bukhari, op. cit.*

Islam has taught us the preciousness of the female at every stage of her life. A believing Muslim's, duty is to live his life in accordance with Islamic teachings, as to please the Creator. If He is pleased with you, then you will benefit, in this life and certainly in the life to come. In order to please Allah, Muslims must follow His commandments. His orders are to be kind and just to women, as daughters, sisters, wives and mothers. Muslim who seek to make their womenfolk happy may expect to earn the pleasure of Allah, and pleasing Allah is the key to Paradise.

> And We have enjoined on man (to be good) to his parents: in travail upon travail did his mother bear him, and in years twain was his weaning: (hear the command), 'Show gratitude to Me and to your parents: to Me is (your final) Goal.
>
> *[Luqman 31:14]*

Although Islam tells us to respect both parents, the mother is given precedence. For months she bears the burden in her womb, sufferings the trials of pregnancy. After the exertion of labour, she suckles the baby for up to two years. She sacrifices her own comforts for the sake of her child. So a man has to recognise, first, the rights that Allah has over him, and then the rights of his parents, especially the mother; he must worship Allah, and occupy himself in obeying and serving his parents to the best of his ability, so long as there is no disobedience to Allah, because Allah's rights are paramount. Everyone must answer to Him, so men and women alike must think of how they will answer to Him for their deeds.[1]

Miqdam ﷺ reported that the Prophet ﷺ said: "O people, listen: Allah the Most High commands you to treat your mothers well. Allah the Most High commands you to be good to your mothers, and thereafter to your fathers".[2] Anas ﷺ reported that the Prophet ﷺ said: "Paradise lies at the feet of mothers". What is meant by this is that a believer may attain the pleasure of Allah, and hence Paradise, by pleasing his mother and attending to her needs. Even if one's

---

[1]   Usmani, *op. cit.*
[2]   *Imam al-Bukhari*, op. cit.

mother is not a Muslim, one is obliged to treat her well and take care of her, so long as this does not entail any disobedience to Allah.

POLYGYNY[1]

The fact that Islam permits a man to have more than one wife (polygyny) has been the cause of much ridicule and misinformation on the part of those who are shallow-minded, prejudiced and inimical towards Islam. They have misled many by publishing and promoting distorted facts and advocating practices that have no basis in the true teachings of the Qur'an and Sunnah.

As we have seen in Chapter I, prior to the advent of Islam, women were treated as chattels and objects for the gratification of men. Girls, women and widows were at the mercy of male whims. In pre-Islamic Arabia, a man could take as many wives as he wanted and treat them as he pleased. In the modern world, this practice continues under the guise of frequent divorces, affairs, mistresses and prostitution. Women are left alone to fend for themselves and their children, whilst divorce is so common that there now exist groups such as "Single Again", which cater for people who have been divorced for the second (or subsequent) time.

Islam did not abolish polygyny, as it recognised that in some cases, polygyny would be necessary and even preferable to the alternatives. However, it strictly limited it, to a maximum of four wives at any one time; there are also stringent conditions to be met by a man who wishes to take a second wife.

The initial intention of this law was to bring some order to the people of Arabia and neighbouring societies, who had been accustomed to unlimited numbers of wives, and to inaugurate a system that would take care of the needs of women, who had been regarded as goods and chattels to be acquired with no regard for their own human feelings. Polygyny also sought to solve the problem of the existence of large numbers of widows and orphans who were left to fend for themselves.

---

[1]   Although the word "polygamy" is the word most commonly used to describe the practice of having more than one wife, the more correct term is "polygyny".

> If you fear that you will not be able to deal justly
> with the orphans, marry women of your choice, two,
> or three, or four; but if you fear that you will not be
> able to deal justly (with them), then only one, or (a
> captive) that your right hands possess. That will be
> more suitable, to prevent you from doing injustice.
>
> *[al-Nisa' 4:3]*

The circumstances in which this *ayah* was revealed illustrate the
sincere teachings of Islam regarding polygyny. It was revealed after
the battle of Uhud, in which a significant number of Muslim men
were martyred and as a consequence, many women were widowed
and their children orphaned. To safeguard the new Muslim
community, this just and compassionate law was revealed, and it
remains in effect until the end of time. Islam requires men to take
full care of the orphan's interests and property, but if they felt that
they could not do justice to them as custodians, then they were advised
to marry other women, up to a maximum of four.

Any man who wishes to take a second wife also has to meet the
important condition of fair treatment of all his wives. The *ayah* quoted
above includes the command to treat wives equally, and anyone who
is unable to do so should marry only one wife. Equal treatment includes
all social, economical and physical needs. It is very difficult for human
beings to be completely fair, a fact which is recognised by the Qur'an:

> You are never able to be fair and just as between
> women, even if it is your ardent desire: but turn
> not away (from a woman) altogether, so as to leave
> her (as it were) hanging (in the air)...
>
> *[al-Nisa' 4:129]*

Shaikh ul Islam of Pakistan, Allamah Usmani suggests that as
equality in all aspects of one's dealings with women is impossible, a
man should do justice as much as is humanly possible. He should
not be excessively inclined towards one wife and disinclined towards
the other and leave her as if she were in suspension. Such an attitude
is cruelty on the part of the husband.[1]

---

[1] Usmani, *op. cit.*

The Prophet ﷺ urged fair treatments of co-wives when he said: "A man who marries more than one woman and then does not deal justly with them will be resurrected with half his faculties paralysed".[1]

It is worth noting that some Muslim "modernists" have linked the two *ayahs* quoted above and drawn the conclusion that Islam effectively allows only one wife, because *al-Nisa'* 4:129 states that it is not possible to treat two women equally, and therefore men who marry more than one woman are put in an impossible position and are acting against Islamic teachings. What the modernists fail to recognise is that the equal treatment referred to is only that which is humanly possible. A man may be more fond of one wife than another, but he is not allowed to make this fact obvious, and he must always ensure that the "less-favoured" wife is taken care of properly. On no occasion did the Prophet ﷺ ever forbid his Companions to take second or subsequent wives. In the case of men who had more than four wives when they embraced Islam, such as Ghaylan ibn Umayyah al-Thaqafi, the Prophet ﷺ asked them to keep four wives and to release the others. The "modernists" have played into the hands of the enemies of Islam by trying to appease non-Muslims and present far fetched interpretations.

Polygyny in Islam is restricted and may be practised only when certain strict conditions are met. It is also the exception rather than the norm in Muslim societies throughout the World. A World Health Organisation census has shown that less than 5% of Muslim men practice polygyny. This is in contrast to other groups in countries such as India, where 15.25% of men from tribal religious groups practise polygyny; 7.97% of Buddhists, 6.72% of Jains and 5.8% of Hindus have plural marriages. The percentage of polygynous marriages in India is lowest among Muslims, at 5.7%.[2]

The figures give an indication of the level of misinformation and stereotyping perpetrated by the Western media. Not only have Westerners coloured themselves with this jaundiced view, but some Muslims are also questioning the teachings of their own religion. It

---

[1]   Imam al-Bukhari, *Sahih al-Bukhari*, op, cit.
[2]   Abdur Rahman I Doi, *Woman in Shari'ah*, Ta-Ha, London. 1989.

is very important for scholars to educate the people and provide them with correct information, to counteract the false picture of Islam and Muslims given by the Western media, and to enable them to understand their own faith more fully.

It is very sad to see the "modernists" propagating monogamy and seeking to change the teachings of the Holy Qur'an by suggesting that polygyny was intended to be practised only in the case of war and the like. These people come up with such pathetic excuses in an attempt to appease the enemies of Islam to no avail.

The topic of polygyny cannot be considered complete without some discussion on the Prophet's ﷺ practice and the historical context in which he and his wives lived. This is a topic which has received much attention from the West, and about which many Muslims are confused. It is a subject which is worthy of an entire book in itself. Here the topic will be covered briefly.

It should be noted that in seventh-century Arabia, adultery, rape and fornication were the norm. Men could have as many wives as they wanted, with no obligation to care for them or attend to their needs as human beings. In this environment, the Prophet ﷺ remained chaste from the beginning. At the age of 25, he married Khadijah ؉, who was a widow 40 years of age and was thus his senior by 15 years. Their marriage was a happy and harmonious one, and remained so until Khadijah passed away some 25 years later. By this time the Prophet ﷺ was 50 years of age and bearing the great responsibility of Prophethood.

The Prophet's ﷺ second wife was Sawdah ؉. She and her husband had been among the earliest converts to Islam. They suffered great hardship at the hands of Quraysh(inhabitants of Mecca), so the Prophet ﷺ had instructed them to migrate to Abyssinia (Ethiopia). There, her husband passed away, and Sawdah suffered much hardship as a widow in a foreign land. The Prophet ﷺ knew that he was responsible for the welfare of his followers, so he proposed marriage to Sawdah. This marriage brought relief, respect and status to her, and provided the Prophet ﷺ with companionship and assistance in raising his children from his marriage to Khadijah. At the time of her marriage to the Prophet ﷺ, Sawdah was around 55 years old.

In order to create blood ties and to show his love and respect to his closest Companions who had given up this world for the sake of Islam, the Prophet ﷺ gave two of his daughters in marriage to Ali ؆ and 'Uthman ؆; he also accepted in marriage 'A'ishah ؆ and Hafsah ؆, the daughters of Abu Bakr ؆ and 'Umar ؆, respectively. His marriage to these two noble women not only enhanced his close ties with his Companions, but these women were later to offer deep insight into the Prophet's ﷺ life. They were responsible for narrating over half of the *ahadith* which now form the basis of the Islamic code of conduct. 'A'ishah ؆ alone is known to have narrated over two thousand *ahadith*.

Zaynab ؆ was a cousin of the Prophet ﷺ. She had previously been married to Zayd ؆, the freed slave and adopted son of the Prophet ﷺ. This marriage had been arranged by the Prophet ﷺ, but the couple were never happy in their marriage and it became apparent that they were not compatible. At the Prophet's ﷺ insistence, they had stayed together for several years, but in the end Zayd could not tolerate it any longer, and decided to set Zaynab free from the marriage contract. The fact that an ex-slave had divorced a woman of the noble Quraysh tribe became the subject of much gossip among the pagans and the weaker members of the Muslim community. Not surprisingly, Zaynab confined herself to her quarters and it fell to the Prophet ﷺ to relieve her of her misery. He married her, and she was around 38 years of age at the time. This action achieved two ends. One was to demonstrate that Islam makes no distinction between class, race or status, as the Qur'an teaches that the noblest person in the sight of Allah is the one who is most pious. The second was to indicate that adopted sons were not to be counted as blood relatives, as had previously been the custom in Arabia.

> ... Nor has He [Allah] made your adopted sons your sons. Such is (only) your (manner of) speech by your mouths. But Allah tells (you) the Truth and He shows the (right) Way.
>
> *[al-Ahzab 33:4]*

In order to unite the tribes of Arabia under Islam, it was deemed necessary to have a blood tie with them, which could be accomplished through marriage. Hence some of the Prophet's ﷺ marriages were arranged to establish inter-tribal ties and to further the cause of unity. The Prophet's ﷺ marriage to Juwayriyah ؇ led to her tribe of Banu Mustaliq, who had been among the fiercest enemies of Islam, freeing all their Muslim prisoners. The whole tribe later entered into Islam. Maymunah ؇ came from the tribe of Najd, who had murdered the emissaries sent to them by the Prophet ﷺ. After his marriage to Maymunah, however, their attitude changed and Najd became favourable towards Islam.

In all, the Prophet ﷺ had eleven wives, of whom two – Khadijah and Zaynab – passed away in his own lifetime. After the *ayah* restricting the number of wives to four was revealed, he contracted no further marriages, but his nine remaining wives were regarded as "mothers of the faithful" and as no other man would be permitted to marry them if he divorced them he kept all his wives on the grounds of compassion.

With the exception of 'A'ishah, all of his wives were widows or divorcees. His marriages were all for political reasons or were contracted in order to set an example of compassion, as in the cases of Zaynab and Sawdah. His polygynous marriage all took place rather late in his life, from the age of 55; taking into account the fact that the responsibility of conveying the message of Islam to the whole of mankind was his to bear, these marriages show the extent of his compassionate and caring nature. He was in a position of great political power, and could have had all the worldly comforts and carnal pleasures had he desired these. However, he chose to marry widows and older women – a sure indication of his upright moral character and desire to set the highest example to his followers.

DIVORCE

The Prophet ﷺ said: "Divorce is the most hateful of all lawful things in the sight of Allah".[1]

---

[1]   Abu Dawood, op, cit.

Although Islam emphasises the importance of marriage, it is a humane and practical religion which recognises the fact that there may be situations in which dissolving the marriage bond may be in the better interests of the individuals concerned and of society at large. Divorce is allowed as a last resort, rather as amputation or major surgery may be the unpleasant but a necessary step needed to save a person's life. If divorce were forbidden, then animosity and adultery may become rampant. To save individuals and society from the greater evils, divorce has been permitted. However, it is not a step to be taken lightly or hastily. Sincere attempts at reconciliation are to be made first and – as in the case of marriage – the rights and welfare of women are to be upheld.

Imam al Ghazzali (b.1058 CE) who is honoured with the title of Hujjat al Islam 'The Proof of Islam' states, the greatest care should be taken to avoid divorce, for, though divorce is permitted, yet Allah disapproves of it. If divorce becomes essential then the woman should be divorced kindly, not through anger or contempt, and not without a valid reason. After divorce a man should give his former wife a present and not announce to others any of her shortcomings.[1]

The Qur'an advises a couple who are facing difficulties in their marriage to appoint arbiters:

> If you fear a breach between them twain, appoint
> (two) arbiters, one from his family and the other
> from hers; if they wish for peace, Allah will cause
> their reconciliation...
>
> *[al-Nisa' 4:35]*

But if the attempts at reconciliation fail, then the couple are permitted to separate,

> But if they disagree (and must part), Allah will
> provide abundance for all from His All-Reaching
> bounty...
>
> *[al-Nisa' 4:130]*

---

[1] Imam al Ghazzali, The Alchemy of Happiness, trans. Claude Field, Octagon Press. London. 1980.

In order to dissolve a marriage, it is essential to pronounce a declaration of *talaq*. There are three types of *talaq* (divorce) that are practised among Muslims.

1 *Talaq ahsan* – (the preferable type of divorce): After issuing one pronouncement of divorce, the couple wait for the *'iddah* (waiting period, which consists of three menstrual cycles of the wife, usually three months). During this time, all possible attempts at reconciliation should be made. The husband may take his wife back at any time during the *'iddah* period. During the period of *iddah* the man must oblige to either keep the woman in the same home or at least furnish her with a comfortable apartment, which is easily accessible to him. Further, the man must provide for her as if no divorce has taken place. At the end of the *iddah* or waiting period if reconciliation has failed then the marriage is broken.

2 *Talaq hasan* – is a divorce where a man pronounces *talaq* to his wife in three consecutive state of purity.

3 *Talaq bid'i* – (bid'i or innovative divorce) is *talaq* where the husband issues three pronouncements of divorce at one time. According to the majority of jurists, this *talaq* is valid but it is against the spirit of the Shari'ah and so the man is an offender in the eyes of the law.

Talaq bid'i is considered a serious act against the Islamic teachings. Hazrat Umar, a close companion of the Prophet ﷺ and the second Calipha of Islam, used to whip the husband who pronounced divorce thrice at one and the same sitting.

> When you divorce women, and they fulfil the term of their ('Iddah), either take them back on equitable terms or set them free on equitable terms; but do not take them back to injure them, (or) to take undue advantage; if any one does that, he wrongs his own soul. Do not treat Allah's Signs as a jest, but solemnly rehearse Allah's favours on you, and the fact that He sent down to you the Book and Wisdom, for your instruction. And fear Allah, and know that Allah is well-acquainted with all things.
>
> *[al-Baqarah 2:231]*

During the *'iddah* period, the couple should stay together, which gives greater opportunity for reconciliation. The woman cannot be evicted from the marital home unless she has committed an indecent act, such as adultery.

> ... And fear Allah, your Lord: and turn them not out of their houses, nor shall they (themselves) leave, except in case they are guilty of some open lewdness, those are limits set by Allah: and any who transgresses the limits of Allah, does verily wrong his (own) soul: you know not if perchance Allah will bring about thereafter some new situation.
>
> *[al-Talaq 65:1]*

When it comes to divorce, Islam treads the middle ground, and safeguards the rights of women. It neither prohibits divorce, thereby imprisoning women as is the case in Hinduism and historical Christianity; neither does it regard divorce as insignificant, as in pre-Islamic Arabia and in the present time.

The right to divorce is not restricted to the husband. The woman may also seek a dissolution of the marriage by means of a process known as *faskh*, whereby she applies to the *Qadi* (Judge) for an annulment of the marriage. The wife may seek *faskh* in several cases, including: apostasy (renunciation of Islam) by the husband; lack of equality of status (*kafa'ah*); lack of compatibility; spoiling of marriage (*fasad*); incurable impotence on the part of the husband and if the husband ill treats the woman (*nushuz*). The above cases present valid grounds for a woman to seek divorce from her husband. If the couple come to a mutual agreement for seperation and get divorced then this is called *khul*.

> If the wife fears cruelty or desertion on her husband's part, there is no blame on them if they arrange an amicable settlement between themselves; and such settlement is best....
>
> *[al-Nisa' 4:128]*

Islam has decreed justice for both sexes in the case of divorce. Although the act of divorce is disliked, it is permitted for the sake of weak human souls who cannot always find comfort and solace in the marriage relationship. This is mainly due to lower tolerance levels, high expectations in others and needless desires.

MODESTY

As already indicated, Islam is a complete way of life, and it has not left out any aspect of human life in its prescription for living. It is to this religion's credit that not only does it point out the dangers of life, but it offers practical solutions to them. One such area is that of modesty, which in the broadest sense means humility, restraint in manner and conduct, avoiding excess and presenting an unpretentious appearance. This is the way of life taught by the Qur'an and exemplified by the Prophet ﷺ.

In humanity, the worst crime after murder is *zina* (adultery), and the punishment dictated by Islam for adultery is equal to that meted out for murder. This indicates the enormity of illicit sexual conduct and the disgust with which this crime is viewed by Islam.

'Abdullah ibn Mas'ud reported, "I asked the Messenger of Allah ﷺ, 'What is the greatest sin?' He replied, 'To set up rivals with Allah by worshipping others although He alone has created you'. I asked, 'What next?' He said, 'To kill your child lest it shouldshare your food'. I asked, 'What next?' He said, 'To commit adultery with the wife of your neighbour'."

The reason behind the prohibition of *zina* is not to "spoil the fun" for people, but because *zina* is the cause of much social chaos, upheaval and suffering for individuals, families, societies and nations. *Zina* destroys the moral fibre of a person, creates an atmosphere of mistrust and deceit, and leads to the birth of illegitimate children who must bear the stigma of their birth. Pornography, prostitution, rape, abortions, divorce and single-parent families are the by-products of *zina*, as is now all too evident in Britain and other Western societies. Families are torn apart, diseases are spread and people's characters become twisted and distorted. The Qur'an warns us:

> Nor come nigh to adultery: for it is a shameful (deed) and an evil, opening the road (to other evils).
>
> *[al-Isra' 17:32]*

To protect the moral well-being of mankind, Islam lays down laws which restrict, if not stop, the things that may lead to *zina*.

> Say to the believing men that they should lower their gaze and guard their modesty: that will make for greater purity for (Amongst) them: and Allah is well acquainted with all that they do.
> And say to the believing women that they should lower their gaze and guard their modesty; that they should not display their beauty and ornaments...
>
> *[al-Nur 24:30-31]*

The first step on the road to *zina* is sight. It is only after a person has had a glance that his desire are inflamed. As men are generally more aggressive in this way, the Qur'an addresses the command of lowering the gaze to the male first. The believing men and women are restricted from gazing at one another, as this is the gateway to greater sin. The Prophet ﷺ said:

> *"the zina of the legs is walking towards an unlawful act, the zina of the hands is touching and patting, and the zina of the eyes is casting passionate glances at those who are forbidden to you".*

Being a practical religion, Islam recognises the fact that a person has to look around to be aware of his or her environment and to see where he or she is going, in which case there is no sin if a person's glance happens to fall upon a person of the opposite sex. It is the second glance which is punishable. The Prophet ﷺ advised Ali,

> *"O Ali, do not allow your first glance to be followed by a second, because the first glance is permitted for you but the second is not".*[1]

---

[1] al-Tirmidhi, *op.cit.*

In other *ahadith*, the Prophet ﷺ warned Muslims against putting themselves into situations where temptation may overwhelm them and the potential for sin is increased:

> *"Let no male stranger sit in privacy with a female stranger, for the third among them is Satan".[1]*
>
> *"Do not go to the houses of women whose husbands are absent".[2]*

There are exceptions to this prohibition on looking at members of the opposite sex. In the case of medical examinations or treatment, deciding on a marriage partner, recording evidence or carrying out criminal investigations, the rulings are relaxed somewhat, but proper conduct and modesty must still be adhered to.

The free mixing of men and women from the time they become sexually aware to the time they are no longer sexually active is prohibited. On the face of it, this may appear rather harsh, but if we examine the effects of unrestricted contact between the sexes, the person who is blessed with understanding and insight will soon see the wisdom behind this restriction. Today, in the Western world, every type of crime that results from free mixing of the sexes is on the increase, as we have seen in Chapter II.

Islamic modesty encompasses not only behaviour, but also dress. It is well-known that appearances count, and that clothes can make a "statement" about the person. Muslims are required to dress modestly and conceal their private parts. The Qur'an reminds us that after the error committed by Adam and Eve, they became aware of their nakedness and shame, so clothing was given as a means of concealing the body:

> O children of Adam! We have bestowed raiment upon you to cover your shame, as well as to be an adornment to you. But the raiment of righteousness - that is the best. Such are among the Signs of Allah, that they may receive admonition!
>
> *[al-A'raf 7:26]*

---

[1] *Ibid.*
[2] *Ibid.*

A prominent commentator, from Asia, on the Holy Qur'an, Hazrat Shah Saheb interprets this ayah as meaning that the enemy (i.e., Satan) stripped them of their 'Paradisian' garments, then Allah taught them the art of dressing, so that henceforth they should wear only the garments of piety.[1]

Allamah Usmani points out that Allah has bestowed many natural resources for human use. He has created cotton, wool, feathers and other materials which man utilises and makes into clothing and other items. When we reflect upon these bounties of Allah, we will easily recognise Allah's favours and become thankful to Him. Moreover, the dress of piety will help us to regain the long-lost Paradisian dress.[2]

Muslims are commanded to cover the *'awrah*, which in the case of men extends from the navel to the knee, and in the case of women includes the whole body except the face, hands and (according to some Hanafi scholars) feet. Muslims should wear clothes that are loose-fitting, thick (non-transparent) and simple (not ostentatious or gaudy).

Although the man's *'awrah* is from the navel to the knee, the *sunnah* (practice) of the Prophet ﷺ is to wear clothes that cover the body from the shoulders to just above the ankles. The *'awrah* is the minimum area to be covered in cases where a person may be too poor to afford more extensive garments.

The guidelines regarding women's dress come straight from the Qur'an:

> And say to the believing women that they should lower their gaze and guard their modesty; that they should not display their beauty and ornaments except what (must ordinarily) appear thereof; that they should draw their veils over their bosoms and not display their beauty except to their husbands, their fathers, their husbands' fathers, their sons, their husbands' sons, their brothers or their

[1] Maulana Abdul Majid Daryabadi, *The Holy Qur'an*, Darul Ishat, Pakistan.
[2] Usmani, *op. cit.*

brothers' sons, or their sisters' sons, or their
women, or the slaves whom their right hands
possess, or male servants free of physical needs,
or small children who have no sense of the shame
of sex; and that they should not strike their feet
in order to draw attention to their hidden
ornaments. And O Believers! Turn all together
towards Allah, that you may attain Bliss.

[al-Nur 24:31]

O Prophet! Tell your wives and daughters, and
the believing women, that they should cast their
outer garments over their persons (when abroad):
that is most convenient, that they should be known
(as such) and not molested. And Allah is Oft-
Forgiving, Most Merciful.

[al-Ahzab 33:59]

The outer garment (*jilbab*) is one which covers a person from head
to foot. A well-known *hadith* further describes the dress of the Muslim
woman: "When a woman reaches the age of maturity, it is not lawful
for her to uncover any part of her body except the face and this -"
and he (the Prophet ﷺ) put his hand on his wrist joint so as to leave
only a little space between the place he gripped and the palm.[1]

Not only do women have to cover themselves in front of men who
are strangers to them, but they are also required to lower their gaze.
Umm Salamah reported that she and Maymunah (who were both
wives of the Prophet ﷺ) were with the Prophet ﷺ when the son of
Umm Maktum, who was blind, came to speak with him. The Prophet
ﷺ told his wives to observe *hijab* in front of the visitor. Umm Salamah
said, "O Messenger of Allah ﷺ, he is a blind man and will not see
us". The Prophet ﷺ said, "He may be blind but you are not, and do
you not see him"?[2]

---

[1]   Sunan Abu Dawood, trans. Prof. Ahmad Hasan, SH Muhammad Ashraf,
       Lahore Pakistan. 1984. Also in Ibn Majah. NOTE – For a proper
       understanding of this hadith a consultation with the Ulama's is requested.
[2]   *Ibid.*

The main aim of *hijab* is to restrain individuals of the opposite sex from being unduly attracted to one another. However, *hijab* has numerous secondary advantages that bring benefits to women. It gives women their own identity and their own sphere, which exists parallel to that of men. Women are thus freed from the strain of Western-style social pressure in which women are expected to look impeccable and sexually attractive at all times, and they are relieved of the "necessity" of spending large amounts of time and money in visiting beauty parlours and applying chemicals, lotions, potions and scents to their bodies for the purposes of gratifying men. Above all, it allows Muslim women to have an identity, an ability to express their personality and intellect of their own, independently of men's whims and desires.

The Prophet ﷺ issued a warning which offers food for thought for all of us:

> *"Those women who appear naked even though they are wearing clothes, who allure and are allured by others, and who walk in a provocative manner, will never enter Paradise, or even smell its fragrance".*[1]

Economics

> And in no way covet those things in which Allah has bestowed His gifts more freely on some of you than on others: to men is allotted what they earn and to women what they earn: but ask Allah of His bounty. For Allah has full knowledge of all things.
>
> *[al-Nisa' 4:32]*

Through Islam, women gained economic liberation and independence from their menfolk. For the first time in human history, Islam bestowed upon women a legal economic entity. A woman could now own, manage, inherit, distribute and sell her own property as she wished and in her own right. Her assets remained hers, and marriage or divorce did not alter the fact. The Islamic ruling and practice with regard to women's economic rights was light-years ahead of any Western equal-rights

---

[1]   Imam Muslim., Sahih Muslim, op,cit.

manifesto. Islam brought these rights to women fourteen hundred years ago, long before equal rights were thought of or campaigned for in other lands.

In the West, women's emergence into the economic arena only took hold during the two World wars when, with most men conscripted for the war effort, the need for labour was so acute that there was no other option but to bring women out of the home. However, it has taken much heartache and a great deal of struggle and striving to bring women anywhere near a position of equal economic status. Even today, the Western woman is economically bound to her husband, who can demand a share from her earnings for ongoing domestic expenses and, in the case of divorce, can claim a share of her savings. In contrast, the Muslim wife is entitled to be supported by her husband, no matter how rich she may be in her own right; whilst she is a child, she is entitled to be supported by her father and in old age she is entitled to be supported by her children. The Muslim woman is relieved of the burden of having to earn a living, and she is allowed to dispose of her earnings in whatever manner she chooses.

In the case of inheritance, the Muslim woman is allotted a share equal to half of that given to her male counterpart. This is often cited as an example of Islam's unfairness to women, but the facts warrant closer examination. In many societies, including pre-Islamic Arabia, wealth that was to be inherited was distributed by means of a written will which in many cases deprived women and those in a weak position of their share; this is still the case in some parts of the world. Islam offers, as it were, a "ready-made will": the Qur'an spells out the Islamic injunctions regarding inheritance, and gives women the right to inherit from husbands, fathers and brothers:

> From what is left by parents and those nearest related there is a share for men and a share for women, whether the property be small or large –
> a determinate share.
>
> *[al-Nisa' 4:7]*

The reason for men being given a portion twice as much as that given to women is that men are responsible for taking care of their womenfolk: A man may be required to spend on his mother, sisters or other female relatives. A woman is entitled to dispose of her share of the inheritance as she wishes, and is under no obligation to support anyone, even herself. When these facts are borne in mind, the just and equitable position of Islam is vindicated.

Islam has given rights to women in all aspects of life, including some where women in other cultures have no rights even today. Many of the instances which critics point to as being unfair to women are, upon closer inspection, found to be favourable to women and may even be seen as giving them preferential treatment.

IV

THE FEMINIST MOVEMENT

It is very important to study and understand the feminist movement, because it claims to represent the emancipation and welfare of women in these times. A need to appraise its logic, practical implications and viability is required, all of which will be addressed in this chapter.

The word "feminism" itself is very subjective and has been used indiscriminately, which has led to a certain measure of confusion and the existence of several definitions. Among the current definitions of feminism are:

- Any groups that have tried to change the position of women, or the ideas about women, have been granted the title of feminist.[1]

- A doctrine advocating social and political rights equal to those of men.[2]

- Feminism means we seek for women the same opportunities and privileges the society gives to men, or that we assert the distinctive value of womanhood against patriarchal denigration. While these positions need not be mutually exclusive, there is a strong tendency to make them so. Either we want to be like men or we don't.[3]

- Feminists must not only work towards the elimination of male privileges but the sex distinction itself; genital differences between human beings would no longer matter culturally. The tyranny of the biological family would be broken and with it the psychology of power.[4]

---

[1]   Olive Banks, *Becoming a Feminist*, Wheatsheaf Books, Brighton, 1986.
[2]   Gerder Lerner, *The Creation of Patriarchy*, Oxford University Press, New York, 1986.
[3]   Judith Evans, Feminist Theory - an introduction to second wave feminism, Sage Publications, California, 1995.
[4]   Shulmith Firestone, The dialectic of sex: the case for feminist revolution, William Morrow & co., New York, 1970.

The emergence of feminism in the West was mainly due to the dual standards of law in favour of men, which were based on the teachings of Christianity. The earliest feminist campaigners demanded an end to the double standard of sexual morality,[1] but this did not mean that they sought an overall lowering of moral standards: the early feminists saw chastity not as oppressive, but as both natural and necessary.

Until fairly recently, Western political systems were open to men only (and there were restrictions on precisely which men were allowed to take part, namely socio-economic class). Women had no say whatsoever. The suffragettes campaigned for women's rights to vote and participate in the political process.

As late as the nineteenth century, oppressive marriage laws were still restricting women with regard to earnings. In the event of a divorce, women were further humiliated by being denied access to their children and being cut off from any source of maintenance. The divorce laws were heavily biased in favour of men.

The development of the factory system drew women out of the home, and the oppression perpetrated by employers who saw women as cheap labour led to the emergence of a women's movement that demanded equal pay and fair treatment. The struggle for equal pay lasted ostensibly until 1975, when a law was finally passed in Britain. However, as women are still being exploited in the work place, and it is not unknown for women to be paid less than men for the same work, the struggle is clearly not yet over.

The existence of all these oppressive laws and practices led to women coming together to demand equal rights and justice. However, as time passed, capitalism and men in positions of power diverted Western women onto a different track. The early feminists' attack on injustice evolved into a movement in which women looked at and accused themselves. So what began with a struggle to change society's (in most cases, men's) attitudes and laws ended up changing women, arguably to the delight of men.

---

[1]   Olive Banks, Faces of Feminism, Martin Robertson, Oxford, 1981.

The feminist movement has become an academic quagmire which has spawned nearly a dozen schools of thought. These may be grouped under the headings of Marxist (or Socialist), Liberal, Sexual and Radical feminism. These will be examined and their theories and practical implications discussed.

MARXIST FEMINISM

The socialist or Marxist tradition has its roots in the works of Karl Marx and Friedrich Engels. However, the idea of socialism predates both, and had already been in circulation among philosophers, economists and politicians. The thought of Marx and Engels is exemplified in the following quotation:

> "As individuals express their life, so they are. What they are, therefore, coincides with their production, both with what they produce and with how they produce. Hence what individuals are depends on the material conditions of their production".[1]

Marx's concept of labour and value may be summarised as follows: The value and power of labour contained within this product can be realized only if others want the commodity – if it has an exchange value in the marketplace. In return for such productive labour, the worker receives a wage, which has within it two components – one a measure of profit or the surplus value appropriated by the capitalist, and the other, the product of necessary labour, is used by the workers to sustain themselves, their family and the next generation.[2] Marx's depiction of capitalism includes a further class, a group which is only tenuously linked to the production process at any given time: the unemployed, the immigrant workers, and *the women* (italics mine). This group comprises various parts of the reserve army of labour ready to be mobilised when production needs to be expanded rapidly, and then demobilised during times of recession.[3]

---

[1]   Sneja Gunew, Feminist Knowledge: critique and construction, Routledge, London, 1990.

[2]   *Ibid.*

[3]   *Ibid.*

Marxist theory emphasises the idea that what makes us human is the fact that we produce our means of subsistence. We are what we are because of what we do or, more specifically, what we do to meet our basic needs in productive activities.[1] What is distinctive about Marxist feminism is that it invites every woman, whether proletarian or bourgeois, to understand women's oppression not so much as the result of the intentional actions of individuals, but as the product of the political, social and economic structures associated with capitalism.[2]

Prior to the introduction of industrial capitalism, the family or household was the site of production. Parents, children and relatives all worked together to produce whatever was needed for the family's survival. Women's work – planting, preserving, canning, cooking, weaving, sewing, childbearing and childrearing – was as essential to the economic activity and success of the family unit as was the work of men. But with industrialisation and the transfer of production from the home to the factory or other public workplace, women – who for the most part did not enter the public workplace, at least in the beginning – came to be viewed as "non-productive," in contrast to "productive" wage-earning men.[3]

This is basically Engels' theory of the cause of women's inferior status, which he blamed on the capitalist system, the family and marriage. In order to bring about an end to the oppression of women, Engels proposed extending legal equality to women and then introducing them *en masse* to the workplace. Such a move would be a prelude to the alliance of all women with the working class to socialise the means of production, abolish private property, and usher in an age of monogamous sexual love.[4]

It was thought that women's primary oppression lay in their role as unpaid domestic workers. This analysis implies that the benefits to

---

[1]   Rosemarie Tong, *Feminist thought: a comprehensive introduction*, Routledge, London, 1989.
[2]   *Ibid.*
[3]   *Ibid.*
[4]   Sneja Gunew, op, cit.

male wage-earners directly offset the disadvantage inherent in their class position. This points to one solution: the abolition of housework as it is now known.[1]

What angered Marxist women most about women under capitalism was the trivialization of women's work. Women were increasingly regarded as mere consumers, as if the role of men was to earn wages and that of women was simply to spend them on "the right products of capitalist industry".[2]

A prominent Marxist feminist, Benston concluded that unless a woman is freed from her heavy burden of domestic duty, including child care, her entrance into the workforce will be a step away from, rather than towards, liberation.[3] Marxist women therefore worked towards moving the women onto the factory work floor and towards earning a living of their own, as a means of proving independence and equality. Another socialist, Warrior, argued that in general, males benefit from women's labour and capitalist males benefit twice. Women are the source of all labour in that they are the producers of all labourers. Their labour creates the first commodity, male and female labourers, who in turn create all other commodities and products. Men, as the ruling class, profit from this commodity through its labour. The male capitalist class makes a profit when it buys this labour power and then receives the surplus value of its visible economic production.[4]

Marxist feminists believe that all women in the capitalist system are subordinate. Middle class women are subordinated in general to the men with whom they live and work, but as members of the middle class they enjoy material and social advantages over both male and female members of the working class. Working class women, on the other hand, bear the dual burden of their subordinate gender and class identities. In the family, as wives and mothers, they are the principal reproducers of the labour power from which capitalism

---

[1] Clare Burton, *Subordination - feminism and social theory*, George Allen & Unwin, Sydney, 1989.
[2] Rosemary Tong op, cit.
[3] *Ibid.*
[4] Clare Burton op, cit..

extracts its surplus, for which service they receive no payment. In addition, many of them, even mothers with children, are in paid employment, which permits the direct extraction of surplus value, while the wages they earn serve to meet family needs, created in increasing number by capitalism itself, for which the income of the male "breadwinner" no longer suffices.[1]

Yet another theory within Marxist feminism suggests that it is not childbearing, physical weakness or any other presumed biologically determined differences that are the basis of women's subordination in capitalist societies; it is the social allocation to women of responsibility for children. The obstacles to changing this connection lie in the capitalist system of production.[2]

In *Capitalism, the family and personal life*, Zaretsky[3] detailed Marxist feminist theory regarding public/private conceptualisation. She argues that patriarchal ideology is vital in the reproduction of capitalism and further that the illusion of a private sphere wherein one's "personal life" is conducted is an integral part of this philosophy. This introduces an entirely new factor: the concept of a personal life, a subjectivity that is self-consciously seeking personal fulfilment. This had not been a factor in the analyses of non-capitalist modes of production. Indeed, one of Zaretsky's arguments is that this search is specific to capitalism.[4]

Zaretsky has two main arguments. The first is that the rise of industrial capitalism promoted a new search for personal identity outside the social division of labour. The second is that the expansion of this "personal life" beyond the place of work created a new basis for women's oppression, since the responsibility for maintaining a refuge from an impersonal society was given to women, or at least to wives and mothers.[5]

Zaretsky traces the particular process of the proletarianization of the petty bourgeoisie, which gave rise to a need for a search for

---

[1]   *Ibid.*
[2]   *Ibid.*
[3]   According to *Ibid.* Eli Zaretsky's Capitalism, the Family and Personal Life 1973 is chosen because it is the best known example of such an approach.
[4]   *Ibid.*
[5]   *Ibid.*

personal identity outside the sphere of work. This became increasingly so as capitalism required a rationalised labour process undisturbed by community sentiment, family responsibilities, personal relations and feelings.[1]

In 1973, Vogel introduced an idea that represented a shift from the original Marxist understanding of domestic work. Vogel wrote: "In short, domestic labour is neither productive nor unproductive... Women's productive activity in the family does not fall under the capitalist mode of production strictly defined. The common characteristic of women, that of being domestic labourers is significant. Thus women who perform domestic labour form a group whose labour is appropriated in a distinct way in capitalist society, in a mode of production whose social relations differ from those of capitalist production. This means that an autonomous women's movement is necessary to represent the oppression which women share as domestic labourers".[2]

What Marxist feminists have tried to highlight is how women's domestic work is trivialised in comparison with wage-earning work, and how women are given the most boring and low-paying jobs.[3]

Dallas Costa published an article 'The Power of Woman and the Subversion of the Community' (1973) which carried an introduction by Selma James and made the unorthodox Marxist claim that women's domestic work is productive not in the colloquial sense of being "useful" but in the strict Marxist sense of creating surplus value.[4] No women have to enter the productive labour force, for all women are already in it, even if no one recognises the fact. Women's work is the necessary condition for all other labour, from which in turn, surplus value is extracted. By providing current (and future) workers not only with food and clothes, but also with emotional and domestic comfort, women keep the cogs of the capitalist machine running.[5]

[1]   *Ibid.*
[2]   *Ibid.*
[3]   Rosemarie Tong, op, cit.
[4]   Clare Burton, op, cit.
[5]   *Ibid.*

Given the view of women's domestic work as productive work, a "wages for housework" campaign painted a picture of women who enter the public workplace as carrying a double load which meant that the day started with paid, recognised work on the assembly line and ended with unpaid, unrecognised work at home. The way to end this inequity, suggested Costa and James, is for women to demand wages for housework. They proposed that the state - not individual men (fathers, husbands) – should pay wages to housewives.[1]

The practical application of Marxism has itself dealt the death blow to its theories, for if Marxism truly intended to save women from oppression, then the people of the Eastern bloc countries would not have risen up as they did in recent years. The failure of Marxism in Eastern Europe is sufficient proof against this theory. However, we should also look at some of the practical issues:

1   Wages for housework is an idea that is neither feasible or desirable as a strategy for the liberation of women. It is not feasible because if the state pays wages to housewives, it will only do so in a way that preserves its own interests. The state would most likely impose a special tax on married men, which would be used to pay wages to their wives. Depending on how large a bite was thus taken out of the husband's income – and there is reason to believe that it would be a hefty sum – the wife's pay cheque would most likely represent nothing more than a rise in status, as there would be no real rise in the family's real income. The housewife's pay cheque would have the further, undesirable, effect of imprisoning women in the home.[2]

2   To regard childbirth as the production of people to be evaluated as a financial asset is a failure to understand and appreciate the value of human beings. In chapter III, we saw numerous *ayat* of the Qur'an and *ahadith* which indicate the higher status of the female due to her gender and unique ability to bring forth and nurture children. Islam has elevated women beyond the narrow, worldly concerns of the workplace and earning a wage, and has

---

[1]   Rosemarie Tong, *op, cit.*
[2]   Tong, *op. cit.*

decreed that her production and nurturing of children gives her a status that equals, if not exceeds, that of men. If Allah and His Prophet ﷺ have told us that the value of a mother is even greater than that of a father, then the status of motherhood must be reinstated to its proper, elevated position.

3 The underlying Marxist theory assumes equality between individuals in terms of financial independence: people are only equal if they earn independently to support themselves. Far from liberating women, Marxism has in fact served the interests of the bosses by supplying them with a surplus of workers which makes it easy for them to demand cheap labour. Real-life experience has shown that few who do get financial independence have gained it by sacrificing their own physical and mental health. However, the majority have become the victims of rather than the winners of the society. From Chapter II we can deduce the ills befalling women in the non Islamic societies of today.

4 Zaretsky suggests that the family is seen as not only a haven for men but also the arena for the personal fulfilment of fathers and husbands, this can only happen at the expense of mothers and wives.[1] This view is contrary to Islamic teachings, which advocates the family as a place where both man and woman obtain serenity and peace. The family thus is the arena which provides both partners with personal fulfilment and protection.

5 The assumption that child-care duties in the home form the basis of oppression implies a need to create communal nurseries, canteens and sleeping quarters. Feminists have falsely assumed that all women would rather be on the shop-floor or in the office than spend time with their children. In fact it is highly improbable that women would like to be whisked straight from the labour ward to the factory floor, thus losing the opportunity to nurture their infants.[2] As far as communal living is concerned, there are not many people who would willingly exchange their privacy and personal space for an open kibbutz-style life. Another consideration

---

[1] Burton, *op.cit.*

[2] Janet Radcliffe Richards, *The Sceptical Feminist*, Routledge & Kegan Paul, London 1980.

is that in a communal environment, it would no doubt be the women who would be employed to take care of the nurseries and canteens, no doubt at unsociable hours and with the lowest status in the hierarchy of roles.[1] (This is in fact the case in many Israeli kibbutzim where women tend to be stuck with the menial tasks and child-care whilst the more interesting and prestigious jobs go to the men).

It may be argued that to expect the state or commune to take care of children is absurd. Since parents choose to have children, they should take the responsibility for their upbringing. If we think of children as valued possessions, we should not say that it is unfair that a family of four should live on the same income as a family of two: we should say that one couple chooses to spend its income on children, whilst the other chooses to spend its money on holidays or furniture.[2] There is no justification for expecting the state to care for children. In a capitalist system, money has become the reward for everything. The feminists have lowered women's value by demanding financial compensation for an asset which they should be proud of.

Marxist theory appears to have little room for questions that deal directly with women's reproductive and sexual concerns: contraception, sterilisation, abortion, pornography, prostitution, rape, sexual harassment and domestic violence.[3]

Marxist feminists try to retain their loyalty to both socialism and feminism. Consequently, they continue to give priority to the issue of class, although – unlike orthodox socialists – they no longer see feminism as a necessary consequence of a socialist victory.[4] They agree, however, that feminism without socialism is impossible (Mitchell, 1971) and for this reason, if no other, the struggle for socialism is given prominence. At the same time, these women find that they can only do so by means of what amounts to a very radical critique of orthodox Marxist views on the position of women.[5]

---

[1] *Ibid.*

[2] Janet Radcliffe Richards, *The sceptical feminist*, Routledge & Kegan Paul, London, 1980.

[3] Tong, *op. cit.*

[4] *Ibid.*

[5] Olive Banks, *Faces of feminism*, Martin Robertson, Oxford, 1981.

If the oppression of women is based on the economic and legal power that men have over them, and if that power is class-based, then it follows that abolishing private property and socialising production destroys the economic foundation of women's position.[1] However, the experience of socialist countries has been used to question this logic.[2] Women under Marxist regimes throughout the world have been the unfortunate victims of oppression in the home, the workplace and in the educational and political spheres. As far as the liberation of women goes, Marxism has offered nothing more than the illusion of justice.

LIBERAL FEMINISM

Liberal feminists see working towards the elimination of the differences between the sexes as the first step towards true equality.[3]

Modern liberal feminist theories of gender equality are based on the assumption that in order to achieve equal status, all stereotyped social roles for men and women have to be abolished. Conventional women's work roles assign to them the major responsibility for unpaid domestic work, especially child care, and thus handicap them with regard to their occupational roles. Despite the legal rights of women to equality in employment, men use women's actual or presumed domestic handicaps to perpetuate *de facto* discrimination by forcing women into a small number of occupational roles that are segregated according to labour market types and working time schedules, and that have lower pay and prestige than comparable men's occupations.[4] Employed women's lower income is used as a justification for the perpetuation of their unequal burden of domestic and child care work and their inferior power in the family. Their segregated and inferior roles also hinder their acquisition of economic and political power. It is in the interests of men of all strata to use the unpaid domestic services of women and prevent women from competing with them for better jobs.[5]

---

[1] *Ibid.*
[2] Gunew, *op. cit.*
[3] Liz Stanley and Sue Wise, *Breaking out again*, Routledge, London, 1993.
[4] Judith Lorber & Susan Farrell, *The Social Construction of Gendrer*, Sage, california, 1991.
[5] *Ibid.*

Liberal feminists seek to create an androgynous individual, that is an individual which would combine some of each of the characteristics, traits, skills and interests that are now stereotypically associated with either men or women.[1] Another goal of the liberal feminists is sexual equality or gender justice, which means freeing women from oppressive roles and enabling them to rise above their lower (or non–existent) position in academia and in the workplace.[2]

These aims raise immediate questions: should women become like men in order to be equal with men? Or should men become like women in order to be equal with women? Or should both men and women lose their identities and become androgynous, each person combining the "correct" blend of positive masculine and feminine characteristics in order to be equal with every other person? The problems thus raised are phenomenal.[3]

It is impossible to create an androgynous individual because of the physical, anatomical, biochemical and physiological differences between the sexes. Another point, made by Ann Ferguson, is that it may not even be desirable for people to be socialised to develop the potential for androgyny. Complete elimination of gender differences raises major legal and economic issues. For example, if a woman is allowed to take six months off work following childbirth, should not the equal male be allowed the same time off to spend time with his new baby? If men and women have the same intellectual capacity and reasoning skills, then surely there is no particular need for female philosophers: men can point out inequities and suggest reforms just as effectively as women.[4]

Liberal feminists seek to prove that women are as good as men. But we may ask: why is this necessary? Why should women have to be like males before they are deemed equal? The direction taken by liberal feminists is destroying the very essence that makes women special.

---

[1] Ann Ferguson, Sexual democracy: women, oppression and revolution, Westview Press, Boulder (Colorado), 1991.

[2] Olive Banks, op, cit.

[3] Tong, *op. cit.*

[4] Evans, *op. cit.*

The oppressive roles from which liberal feminists seek to free women are not confined only to females. The immigrant population, male and female alike, are the worst victims of oppression; but even Caucasian males may be discriminated against in the case of jobs such as child-care and secretarial work, which are "reserved" for females. No doubt women suffer more than men, but they cannot be seen as unique when ethnic minorities and immigrants in the Western world are also suffering oppression.[1] The roots of this inequity lie in capitalism and its need to seek cheap labour in order to increase returns on investment.

Elshtain, a critic of liberal feminism, states that "there is no way to create real communities out of an aggregate of freely choosing adults". She argues that liberal feminists have over-emphasised the male up to the point of equating masculinity with humanity, manly virtues with human virtues. She argues that liberal feminism has three major flaws: the assumption that women can become like men if they set their minds to it, the notion that all women want to become like men, and the claim that all women should want to become like men and to aspire to masculine values.[2]

Liberal feminism has a tendency to over-estimate the number of women who want to be like men, who want to abandon the role of wife and mother for that of citizen and worker. Any woman whose identity is that of a wife and mother is likely to become angry or depressed when, after years of investing blood, sweat and tears, she is told that being a wife or a mother is a mere role, and a problematic one at that. It is one thing to tell a woman to change her hairstyle; it is something else altogether to tell her that she should get a more meaningful identity.[3]

A profound statement by Elshtain states that liberal feminists are wrong to advocate that women should reject traditional values. Articles written for women about dressing for success, making it in a man's world, being careful not to cry in public, avoiding intimate

---

[1]   Ann Ferguson, *op. cit.*
[2]   Tong *op. cit.*
[3]   *Ibid.*

friendship, being assertive, and playing hardball serve only to erode what after all may be best about women.[1] It is wrong to assume that women must be the same as men in order to be socially, economically or politically equal. In fact the sexes can be different, carry out different tasks, and still be equal on all these levels.[2]

From the Islamic point of view, there is no room for entertaining a desire to create androgynous individuals. If the Creator had intended this for us, He could have created us as asexual beings who would reproduce like the hydra. However, the issue of oppression of others on the basis of their sex or skin colour still needs to be addressed. Equal opportunities and equal pay must be implemented for all, without bias. Laws should be instituted that would guarantee such equality, whilst taking into account any physical differences and ruling in favour of the weaker individuals. As stated earlier, the Qur'an tells us that Allah has assigned to the male his duties and to the female hers. The Prophet ﷺ is reported to have said: "Allah's curse is upon those men who imitate women and those women who imitate men".[3]

RADICAL FEMINISM

The *New York Feminist Manifesto* of 1971 declares:[4]

"Radical feminism recognises the oppression of women as a fundamental political oppression wherein women are categorised as an inferior class based upon their sex. It is the aim of radical feminism to organise politically to destroy this sex class system. As radical feminists we recognise that we are engaged in a power struggle with men, and that the agent of our oppression is man in so far as he is identified with and carries out the supremacy privileges of the male role. For while we realise that the liberation of women will ultimately mean the liberation of men from their

[1] *Ibid.*
[2] Alice Rossi, A biosocial perspective on parenting.
[3] Imam al-Bukhari.
[4] Clare Burton, *op. cit.*

destructive role as oppressor, we have no illusions
that men will welcome this liberation without
struggle. Radical feminism is political because it
recognises that a group of individuals - men - have
set up institutions throughout society to maintain
this power".

Radical, or extreme, feminism regards men as evil, benefiting from
their power over women in every way, from ego-satisfaction, economic
and domestic exploitation, sexual domination and political power.[1]

Many radical feminists argue that in order to make a complete
commitment to feminism, a woman has to be or become a lesbian. A
leading radical feminist, Bunch believed that only lesbians can be
serious feminists, and that lesbianism is best understood as a
revolutionary rejection of all males and male-defined institutions.[2]

Adrienne Rich suggested that compulsory heterosexuality is the
central social structure perpetuating male domination.[3] A refusal of
heterosexuality acts as an underground feminist resistance to
patriarchy. She defines a lesbian as a woman bonded primarily to
women who is sexually and emotionally independent of men.[4]

Rich's "lesbian continuum" proposes that all women are lesbians,
insofar as they want to identify with other women.[5] She makes two
basic assumptions in her defence of the lesbian continuum as a
construct for understanding female resistance to patriarchy. First,
she assumes that compulsory heterosexuality is the key mechanism
underlying and perpetuating male dominance; second, she implies
that all heterosexual relations are coercive in nature.[6] Radical
feminists allege that marriage is at the root of women's subjection to
men because through it, men control both a woman's reproduction
and her person.[7] Marriage is thus seen as slavery for women, without

---

[1]   Michele Barrett, *Women's oppression today*, Verso, London, 1980.
[2]   Tong, *op. cit.*
[3]   Ann Ferguson, *op. cit.*
[4]   *Ibid.*
[5]   Evans, *op. cit.*
[6]   Ann Ferguson, *op. cit.*
[7]   Banks, *op. cit.*

the abolition of which freedom for women cannot be won. A prominent feminist philosopher, De Beauvoir stated, "Women pay for their happiness with their freedom". She insisted that this price is too high for anyone because the kind of contentment, tranquillity and security that marriage offers a woman drain her soul of its capacity for greatness.[1]

The effect of removing men from the scene altogether is not only weakening traditional male/female tie, if not destroying it altogether, but the bond between father and child is eliminated. Meanwhile, the tendency for men to become merely temporary sexual partners and to lose their parental role increases. Instead of making men responsible and share in the duties of nurturing children, women are inadvertently freeing men of all responsibilities, no doubt to the great delight of capricious men.

Radical feminism's main aim is the destruction of patriarchy, which Ruth Blair defines as: "the historic system of male dominance, a system committed to the maintenance and reinforcement of male hegemony in all aspects of life – personal and private privilege and power as well as public privilege and power".

Gerder Lerner defines it more clearly:

> "Patriarchy means the manifestation and institutionalisation of male dominance over women and children in the family and the extension of male dominance over women in society in general..".

Patriarchy is a system of structures and institutions created by men in order to sustain and recreate male power and female subordination. Such structures include institutions such as law, religion and the family; ideologies which perpetuate the naturally inferior position of women; socialisation processes which ensure that women and men develop behaviour and belief systems appropriate to the powerful or powerless group to which they belong.[2]

---

[1] Rosemarie Tong, *op. cit.*
[2] Gunew, *op. cit.*

Patriarchy also has a materialistic base - the economic systems are structured so that women have difficulty getting paid labour in a society which values only paid labour and in which money is the currency of power. Women without economic independence cannot sustain themselves without a breadwinner: they cannot leave a brutal husband, they cannot withdraw sexual, emotional and physical servicing from men, they cannot have an equal say in decisions affecting their own lives, such as where they might live. Radical feminism has therefore stressed the necessity of women exercising economic power in their own lives.[1]

Charlotte Buch has emphasised the importance of class analysis in radical feminism. In her words:

> "Women's oppression is rooted both in the structure of our society, which is patriarchal, and in the sons of patriarchy: capitalism and white supremacy. Patriarchy includes not only male rule but also heterosexual imperialism and sexism; patriarchy led to the development of white supremacy and capitalism. For me, the term patriarchy refers to all these forms of oppression and domination, all of which must be ended before all women will be free".

Arguments from within the feminist group state that absolute separatism from men is neither feasible nor desirable. It is not desirable because "women will destroy patriarchy by confronting it, not by isolating themselves from it".[2]

One of the first radical feminists to gain prominence was Shulamith Firestone, who wrote:

> "The end goal of feminist revolution must be not just the elimination of male privilege but of the sex distinction itself. Genital differences between human beings would no longer matter culturally. The tyranny of the biological family would be broken and with it the psychology of power".

---

[1]   *Ibid.*
[2]   Tong, *op. cit.*

For Firestone it is from sexual differences that women's subordination sprang, in part, as reproductive biology condemned women to a fearful existence of bearing children, to be oppressed, in squalor and in pain.[1] Firestone states: "Nature produced the fundamental inequality which was later consolidated and institutionalised in the interests of men".[2] In this account, the reproductive bond is not even remotely pleasing; it is wretched. Firestone then draws the logical conclusion to such an opinion: she proposes freeing women from their long ordeal by means of changes in reproductive technology that would allow women to avoid pregnancy and childbirth - just as is happening now:

> "Until the taboo is lifted, until the decision not to
> have children or not to have them naturally is at
> least as legitimate as natural childbearing, women
> are being forced into their female roles".

Therefore, according to this way of thinking, women must rebel. Women must control fertility. Women must own their bodies and new technology. Above all, women must control childbirth and childrearing. In Firestone's view, this "natural" inequality can only be overcome when there is a complete separation of reproduction from women's lives, so that women and men are made equal through technological innovations. Technology that will allow artificial reproduction outside women's bodies must be developed.[3]

Whilst some radical feminists like Firestone want to free women from biological maternity, there is another version of feminism that wants to free maternity from male domination.[4] This thesis describes and deplores the transfer of maternity care from women (midwives) to men (male obstetricians) that has occurred in the West over the past century or so. This liberation of maternity from male domination entails the return of childbirth to the care of women themselves, but for many feminists it also includes the progressive removal of the rights and duties of fatherhood.

[1] Judith Evans, *op. cit.*
[2] Burton, *op. cit.*
[3] *Ibid.*
[4] Olive Banks, *op. cit.*

If men in themselves were the enemy, as many radical feminists believe, then the solution could well come to be the abolition not only of marriage or even of the family, but of men themselves,[1] whether by their exclusion from women's society or by more extreme means. It is not likely that many women in the movement envisaged the physical destruction of men, and certainly it is difficult to see this as a practical possibility.[2]

Many feminist theories suggest that men have conditioned women and have taken control over them. Feminists thus ignore the views of the majority of women by assuming that women have let their minds be manipulated by men and are not capable of deciding what is best for themselves. But if feminists believe that women are weak and stupid enough to be conditioned by men, then it follows that if women follow their ideologies, then they have merely exchanged one type of coercion for another.[3]

Feminists object to the allocation of gender roles, and complain if men and women are expected to do different sorts of work solely on the basis of their sex. But if, like the feminists, we go to the extreme of assuming that we have not rid ourselves of tyranny until men and women are doing the same sort of work, we risk a different problem, that of forcing them to do the same things although the majority may have the inclination to do different things.[4]

Feminists object to sexism although the majority of people see gender as relevant. When there are fewer women in certain positions on the career ladder, it is the feminists who are quick to point out sex differences.

Firestone's suggestion that reproduction must take place outside of women's bodies before women are liberated is senseless. If any advances in "test tube" reproduction are made, the technology will no doubt be under the control of males. It is true to say that radical feminism is not practical and would not survive for long if it were implemented: If heterosexuality were halted, this would prevent

---

[1] *Ibid.*
[2] *Ibid.*
[3] Janet Radcliffe Richards, *op. cit.*
[4] Richards, *op. cit.*

the production of a new generation and the human race would come to an end. Some might suggest that children could be produced by means of artificial insemination or cloning. For women to totally succeed in this they will no doubt be confronted by men, who will rightly fight for their survival. It cannot be envisaged even by the most ardent feminist, that the battle of sexes should led to the battle fields of war. It is in fact absurd to regard men as the core of evil, because there is no real benefit for men as a whole in suppressing women. Men have to co-habit with women, and most sane human beings of either gender would prefer to live in peace and harmony with their spouses, the "battle of the sexes" makes no sense at all.

Research has shown that the majority of lesbians go under the banner of feminism, and that they represent around 10% of active feminists.[1] In this case it appears that some women have used feminism as a guise to fulfil their deviant sexual desires. Homosexuality is completely forbidden in Islam, and there is no room for "gay" religious movements such as those that have emerged in Christianity. Homosexuality represents something which is at odds with the natural order and endangers the stability of human society.[2]

> Would you really approach men in your lusts rather than women? Nay, you are a people (grossly) ignorant!
>
> *[al-Naml 27:55]*

The Qur'anic view (which, by the way, coincides with that of the Bible, e.g. Leviticus 20:13) is that homosexuality is an abomination and that those who indulge in it are "committing excesses". This includes both male and female homosexuals, or "gays" and "lesbians" as they are known.

Radical feminists assume that all marital relations are coercive. This undermines women and implies that they are not capable of taking care of themselves, but need a "big sister" in an ivory tower to think for them. Radical feminism gives women less credit than they deserve.

---

1   Ann Ferguson, *op. cit.*
2   Abdul Wahid Hamid, *Islam: The Natural Way,* MELS, London, 1989.

To propagate a complete ban on marriage would throw the world into disarray. Even if all individuals did not become homosexuals, we would find ourselves with a completely promiscuous society. An individual is not always attracted to a person who likes him or her, so with no moral restraints, those who are physically, economically and socially strong would fulfil their carnal desires at the expense of the weak. Incest and paedophilia would become rife. It would be a nightmarish society in which exploitation of women would be the order to the day.

Most of those who have examined the development of radical feminism are agreed that it has been seriously weakened by internal disputes, by its lack of formal structure, and by the inherent weaknesses of its theories. Its heyday was in the late 1960s, but since the 1970s it has fallen into a decline with its most committed followers retreating into communes where they could practise no more than a kind of personal redemption.[1]

SEXUAL LIBERATION

Mitchell suggested that women's status and function are jointly determined by her role in production, reproduction and the socialisation of children and sexuality.[2]

To determine which of these factors most oppress women, Mitchell came to the conclusion that women are making progress only in the area of sexuality. Taken to extremes, sexual liberation becomes merely another form of sexual oppression. In the past, women were condemned for being whores; now they are condemned for being virgins.[3] Curiously, a British newspaper report on female converts to Islam asked "Why are British women finding true sexual freedom in Islam"? This sensationalist piece of rhetoric turned out to refer to the refreshing freedom from the sexual pressure which is so prevalent in Western society.[4]

---

[1]   Banks, *op. cit.*
[2]   *Ibid.*
[3]   Tong, *op. cit.*
[4]   "Why are British women turning to Mecca"? Daily Mail, December 2, 1993

Not everyone concerned with human liberation welcomed the liberation of sexuality. Marxist philosophers argued that it was a device to distract people from more serious political and economical oppression. Other feminists said that the liberation of female sexuality brought a reinforcement of the image of creatures of a separate and powerless sphere. The Victorian stereotype of feminine purity at least had the merit of rendering women special in the eyes of men. In the pursuit of equality and freedom even this dubious moral advantage was lost, and the way was opened for a new and less advantageous stereotype. It was no accident that the most ardent supporters of the "playboy" style of sexual liberation were men![1]

A woman may say that she diets, exercises and dresses for herself, but in reality she is most likely to be shaping and adorning her body for the benefit of men. A woman has little or no say about where, when, how or by whom her body will be used, because it can be appropriated through acts that range from standing on the corner "watching all the girls go by" to the extreme of rape.[2] In contrast, women's progress in the area of reproduction, production and socialising of children has, according to Mitchell, ground to a halt.[3]

Islam finds the whole idea of promoting sex for pleasure to be totally distasteful – as do many rational individuals who live in the West. Casual approaches to sex, such as "cruising" or using pornography are identified as being male-oriented, since they focus on sex for physical pleasure rather than as a means of deepening emotional intimacy and affection.[4] Seeking sex only for physical pleasure is dehumanising, because it treats people only as sexual objects and fails to tap the potential of the act for a deeper meaning, which is an intimate knowledge of and commitment to another human being.[5]

The feminist drive towards sexual liberation has had catastrophic consequences for women's social status. As we have already seen in

---

[1] David Boucher, The feminist challenge: the movement for women's liberation in Britain and America, Macmillan, 1983.
[2] Tong, *op. cit.*
[3] *Ibid.*
[4] Ann Ferguson, *op. cit.*
[5] Abdul Wahid Hamid, *op. cit.*

Chapter II, the push for women's equality in the West has been accompanied by an increase among females of all the vices formerly associated with men. Alcoholism, smoking, gambling and criminal activity have all increased and are as likely to be found among females as among males. In early 1996, it was announced that the female prison population in the UK had increased by 30% in the previous year alone.

For many women, their new "freedom" has brought the dismal experiences of exploitation, abandonment by men, abortions, financial hardships, single parenthood and isolation. The sexual liberation movement has resulted in increased social, financial, health and economical hardship. Overall the greater sexual freedom is being acknowledged as working in favour of men rather than women.

APPRAISAL

All branches of feminism have their shortcomings, and the movement has essentially failed to address issues facing all the women throughout the world. Marxist theory has ignored the issues of oppression of women via pornography, prostitution and sexual harassment. Radical feminism has only served the interests of a few women living in Western suburbia, and its theories are inherently weak, as has been shown. Sexual feminism has only served to wet male appetites and has plunged the women of the West into the worst form of oppression since the *Jahiliyyah*. The failure of feminist ideologies to truly liberate women should come as no surprise, since these are based on theories which have been devised by humans for humans: as such they will undoubtedly contain factors that will please some, displease others, and ignore the majority. The solutions to human problems can only come from the Creator of humans. It is to Him that we must turn, and it is in His teachings alone that we will find true liberty for all human beings.

The feminists have given women laws against sexual discrimination and equal opportunities in the fields of education and work, which are undoubtedly deserved and which Islam would certainly condone. However, as feminism succeeded in freeing women from the oppression of law and domesticity, a more sinister form of oppression, in the form of the tyranny of "beauty", took over. This phenomenon is described by Naomi Wolf as the "beauty myth".

THE TYRANNY OF "BEAUTY"

The "Rites" of beauty are able to isolate women so well because it is not yet publicly recognised that the devotees of beauty are trapped in anything more serious than fashion and a private distortion of self-image.[1] The Rites took over women's minds, in the wake of the women's movement, because oppression, like nature, abhors a vacuum; they gave back to women what they had lost when faith in God died in the West.[2] The swift spread of this new "religion" was ably assisted by the capitalist industries. Now, rather than being assessed on their personal, intellectual and professional merits, women are judged by their physical attributes. This abhorrent attitude is diametrically opposed to Islam, which directs people's attention towards an individual's character by asking them to base their respect on the level of a person's piety.

Until recently, pornography was only for male consumption. However, the feminists have fallen into the trap that was carefully laid by those who had a vested interest in making women believe it is normal for a liberated women to enjoy pornography. Pornography, which never depicts legal, intimate love between married couples, has the pernicious effect of planting notions of the acceptability of adultery, fornication and rape in idle minds.[3] Film, TV and printed media find themselves in direct competition with pornography, which is now the biggest media category worldwide, so the images of women and beauty in those media become more extreme. Incredibly, pornography generates an estimated $7 billion a year, more than the legitimate film and music industries put together. Pornographic films outnumber other genres by three to one. Researchers report that pornography worldwide is becoming increasingly violent [4] and "snuff" movies which record the ordeal of real victims are not uncommon.

---

[1] Naomi Wolf, *The beauty myth*, Vintage(Chatto & Windus), London, 1991.
[2] *Ibid.*
[3] *Ibid.*
[4] *Ibid.*

Beauty became the currency of exchange and, like money, was highly sought after by women. However, it was more elusive than pound notes or dollar bills, as men kept devaluing the "currency". There are no universal standards: "beauty" is an imaginary idol created by the Western male, who raises and changes its standards at whim, thereby making it impossible for his mother, sister or daughter to attain it. Women's beauty has nothing to do with women: it is all about men's institutions and power. In the West, the man's right to pass judgement on any woman's appearance without himself being subjected to scrutiny is regarded as God-given.[1]

As the white middle-class women threw away their aprons and marched out of their front doors in pursuit of liberation, they fell straight into the trap of the capitalist beauty parlour. The capitalist market has manipulated women to spend over $33 billion a year on diet products, $20 billion on cosmetics, $300 million on cosmetic surgery, and over $7 billion on pornography.[2]

The consequent burden of oppression borne by women is immense, of which the following represent only the tip of the iceberg:

1   The most obvious effect is the vast amount of time, effort and money which women are expected to devote to their appearance whilst no such demands are made of men.[3]

2   The standards that women are expected to attain are impossible, because the goal posts are constantly being shifted. The media must take the lion's share of the blame for this problem.

3   At any given time, the standards of beauty are limited and rigid, and exclude the majority of ordinary women. Whatever body shape is dictated to be "fashionable," those whose natural appearance differs from it will never be able to attain it and risk subsequent low self-esteem and depression, etc.[4]

---

[1]   *Ibid.*
[2]   *Ibid.*
[3]   Richards, *op. cit.*
[4]   *Ibid.*

4   The fashion industry pressurises women to fight their own natural bodies by undergoing cosmetic surgery, squeezing themselves into tight dresses and skirts, crippling their feet with stiletto heeled shoes and starving themselves into ill-health in the name of dieting.

This is what feminism has achieved, instead of protesting against male demands that women should essentially be sensual and pleasing to men. The feminist movement has found its greatest support among capitalist corporate companies and "playboy" type men.

The demands of the beauty myth are destroying women, morally, psychologically and spiritually. Women need to emancipate themselves from this unjust demand made by male driven society. In order to achieve this it is not lobbying or government bills that are needed but a need to revert to a philosophy that frees them from the tyranny of fashion and role models, a philosophy that appreciates a woman for herself and judges her on her character, and not for her beauty or bank balance, a philosophy that will reinstate her personal identity and self-respect. This is to be found only in Islam.

The sociologist Deborah L. Sheppard states:

> "Women perceive themselves and other women to be confronting constantly the dualistic experience of being feminine and businesslike at the same time while they do not perceive men experiencing the same contradiction".

Women are encouraged by advertisers to wear clothes that express their femininity yet maintain business-like looks. By this they mean women wear clothes that reveal their breasts, thighs and lace-lined lingerie. Women are caught between the conflicting ideals of "businesslike" and "feminine", and suffer as a result. Over 75% of women experience harassment that they blame on themselves and their poor control over their appearance. Five studies on sexual organisation have found that "a woman's behaviour is noticed and labelled sexual even if it is not intended as such". Women's friendly actions are misinterpreted as sexual.[1] This is substantiated by the

---

[1]   *Ibid.*

fact that 38% of men have been found to abuse their power in the work place to rape women.[1] Islam clearly teaches Muslims to avoid creating or entering such freely-mixed environments in the first place, which prevents such misery and suffering from occurring.

The fashion industries dependency on survival by exploiting women can be assessed by the reaction of the industry to John Molloy's best seller book, *Women's dress for success*, advocating women to wear a uniform at work. This minor observation made by Molloy led the New York Times magazine, whose financial survival depends on the advertising revenue of the beauty industry, to publish an article declaring Molloy's views as passé. Other media, who received a sizeable portion of their advertising funds from the fashion industry quickly followed suit.[2] From all of this, one can understand why Islam, which preaches moderation and simplicity in dress and lifestyle is facing such hostility from the capitalist world.

If working women did not dress up like models, the secret pleasures enjoyed by their male colleagues may decrease. No doubt if women followed Islamic standards of dress and conduct, the incidence of sexual harassment would be negligible and women would be spared a major source of oppression. Above and beyond that women's character would not be passed on sexual appeal but her intellect and ability.

From the 60's onwards the fashion industry, with capital growth interest at heart, have used the media to manipulated women in thinking nudity and low weight are an expression of liberation. Between 1968 and 1972, the number of diet-related articles rose by 70%. Articles on dieting in the popular press soared from 60 in the whole year of 1979 to 66 in the month of January 1980 alone. By 1984, 300 diet books were on the shelves of bookstores. The lucrative "transfer of guilt" was achieved just in time.[3]

The paranoia with weight in women has began to appear at a very early age and consequently claims many victims. Anorexia and Bulimia are overwhelmingly female maladies: between 90 and 95%

---

[1] Tong, *op. cit.*
[2] *Ibid.*
[3] Wolf, *op. cit.*

of sufferers are women. America, which has the greatest number of women who have "made it" in the male world, also leads the world with regard to rates of female Anorexia. The American Anorexia and Bulimia Association states that Anorexia and Bulimia strike one million US women every year. Every year, 150,000 American women die of Anorexia. Brumberg reports that between 5 to 15% of hospitalised anorexics die during treatment, giving this disease one of the highest fatality rates for mental illness.[1]

The UK now has 3.5 million anorexics or bulimics, with 6,000 new cases yearly. Another study of adolescent British girls shows that 1% are now anorexic. According to the women's press, at least 50% of British women suffer eating disorders.[2]

As the females began to integrate with the males, in all the spheres, women's body shape and size began to play a prominent role in an oppressing way to the women. A generation ago, the average model weighed 8% less than the average American woman; today she weighs 23% less.[3]

A 1985 survey showed that 90% of respondents thought they weighed too much. Although today's girls have inherited the gains of the women's movement, in terms of personal distress they are no better off. Fifty-three percent of high school girls are reported to be unhappy with their bodies by age 13, and by age 18, over 78% are dissatisfied. The feminist movement has created the hunger cult which is striking a major blow against women's fight for equality.[4]

In the West, female bodies have become public property and female "fat" is the subject of intense public debate. Women feel guilty about female fat because they are made to believe that their bodies belong not to them, but to society. Thinness is not a private ascetic but a hunger, a social concession exacted by the community. A cultural fixation on female thinness is not an obsession about female beauty but an obsession about female subservience.[5]

---

[1] *Ibid.*
[2] *Ibid.*
[3] *Ibid.*
[4] *Ibid.*
[5] *Ibid.*

Women's images in the media and magazines are glamorised by "retouching" or "computer imaging" so that a 50 year old woman looks 30 and a 65 year old looks 45. Bob Ciano, an art director at *Life* magazine, says that, "no picture of a woman goes unretouched... Even a well-known older woman who doesn't want to be retouched... We still persist in trying to make her look like she's in her fifties". The effect of this censorship according to Heyn is clear: "by now readers have no idea what a real woman's 60 year old face looks like in print because it's made to look 45. Worse, 60 year old readers look in the mirror and think they look too old, because they are comparing themselves to some retouched face smiling back at them from a magazine. Women's culture is an adulterated, inhibited medium".[1] How do the values of the West, which hates censorship and believes in a free exchange of ideas, fit in here?[2]

This issue is not trivial. It is about the most fundamental freedoms: the freedom to imagine one's own future and to be proud of one's life. Airbrushing age from women's faces has the same political echo as making black people look white: it is condescending, insulting and offensive. To make women look younger, thinner and more curvaceous is to erase women's true identity, worth, power and history. This is the most damaging type of oppression and women in the West are slowly waking up to it.[3] This is one reason why young educated women in the West have found the sincere teachings of Islam to be so attractive.

Magazines and other media are under pressure to project the idea that looking one's age is undesirable because their survival in the capitalist society depends on their advertising revenue. In the US alone, 65 million dollars' worth of advertising revenue comes from companies who would go out of business if looking one's age was acceptable or desirable.[4] It is in the interest of companies that reap wealth from women to make them feel inferior about their bodies. Through the media the message is hammered in daily. As women

---

[1]   *Ibid.*
[2]   *Ibid.*
[3]   *Ibid.*
[4]   *Ibid.*

spend millions of Pounds and hours worldwide, on 'beauty' products and go through dangerous and painful procedures to look like the way they have been indoctrinated by the media. If only women wake up to their own worth which Allah has favoured them with, the companies via the media will continue to exploit them and the problem is going to escalate.

Young women's oppression is one story, but as women get older their miseries in the West simply multiply. Old women are not only poorer, but they are also neglected, by the state and by their own children. Western culture is such that helpless older people are left out of sight in public nursing homes, and young children are kept out of their parents' sight in nurseries and day-care centres. The West is rapidly moving towards a system where it is only worth living if you are able to fend for yourself in all aspects. Thus the value of individuals is only measured in terms of supplying society either with surplus labour or beauty. Hence the young who cannot provide the capitalist economy with surplus value and the old who are no longer aesthetically pleasing are excluded from mainstream society and locked away in nurseries and old peoples' homes respectively. Old age carries such a stigma in the West that adult children may be reluctant to be seen with their ageing and ailing parents in public. The very parents who nursed us and wiped our bottoms when we had no faculty of reasoning have now become a burden. In contrast, Islam urges those who are strong and in good health to take care of the infirm, and specifically makes it a duty upon the children to take care of their ageing parents and not even to speak to them in a loud or angry voice.

> Thy Lord hath decreed that ye worsh00ip none but Him, and that ye be kind to parents. Whether one or both of them attain old age in thy life, say not to them a word of contempt, nor repel them but address them, in terms of honour.
>
> *[Banu Israil 17 : 23]*

> We have enjoined on man kindness to his parents: In pain did his mother bear him and in pain did she give birth.
>
> *[Al-Ahqaf 46 : 15]*

(see also *Luqman 31:14* quoted earlier and *Al Ankabut 29:8, Al-Ahqaf 46: 16, 17, 18*)

The average American old woman's income is half that of an old man. In Britain, old women outnumber old men by four to one, and of those twice as many old women as old men rely on income support (government assistance). Signs of ageing are viewed by Western women as a calamity, and women are constantly harangued in the media about the awfulness of wrinkles, grey hair and sagging breasts. The solution offered is: beauty parlours and plastic surgery, which is so risky and painful that it may be placed on a par with slavery. Modern cosmetic surgeons have a vested financial interest in a social role for women that requires them to feel ugly. The cosmetic surgery industry in the US grosses $300 million annually, and is growing at a yearly rate of 10%. Between 200,000 and 1 million American women have had their breasts cut open and sacs of chemical gel implanted.[1]

The effects of feminism have been so devastating that women would do themselves a great favour if they were to abandon it and begin enjoying the pleasures that the Creator has given them. Food is a bounty from Allah from which women may eat what is good for them and enjoy it. Women's bodies are for themselves, not for public display: they should stop pandering to society's pleasure and bowing to the demands of the fashion industry. Women should bear the signs of ageing with pride, as marks of seniority and wisdom.

> ... These are the limits ordained by Allah; so do not transgress them. If any do transgress the limits ordained by Allah, such persons wrong (themselves as well as others).
>
> *[al-Baqarah 2:229]*

---

[1]   *Ibid.*

CONCLUSION

Islam forbids the one thing that modern men and women have excelled in: a laissez-faire society. In contrast, Islam commends chastity, marriage, reproduction and upbringing of children, all of which the "modern, liberated women" has been encouraged to abandon, at her peril.

Sex, in Islam, is permitted only within wedlock, a measure which protects women from being used and abused. This also puts sex into its proper place in relation to other human needs such as social comfort, security and companionship. In Islam, sex is not the be-all and end-all of life, but it is an important ingredient for a harmonious, caring and mutually supportive relationship between a married couple. It is a means of deepening love, affection and consideration towards one another.

The prominent feminist philosopher Simone de Beauvoir considered the roles of wife and mother to be a hindrance to women's freedom, and believed that women could only escape the trap of femininity by assuming the role of a professional career women. But it turns out that even the career woman cannot escape the cage of femininity, indeed she has it much worse because she faces pressure to appear and act feminine as well as to succeed in her chosen career.[1]

Many feminists seek to steer women away from marriage and childbearing, as if women were unable to find happiness in these. It is a sign of arrogance on the part of feminists to make such assumptions. Even worse, they contend that those women who have found happiness and security in marriage are only fooling themselves.

Although in the early part of the twentieth century, feminist efforts focused on the campaign for women's suffrage and its consequences, a much greater impact on women's lives came from changes that had less to do directly with the women's movement, and everything to do with a loosening of morals and manners.[2] After the First World War, there was an increase in literature on female sexuality and

[1]   Rosemarie Tong, *op. cit.*
[2]   Olive Banks, *op. cit.*

premarital sex, which had an effect on society. Whereas it had previously been the males who were immoral, women now – instead of demanding moral behaviour from the males – began to follow the male lead in immorality, to the delight of many men. The feminist movement, which supposedly liberated women, gave men the greatest pleasure. Not only has feminism allowed men to satisfy themselves sexually, but they are now in a position to demand that women look the way they want them to, based on the fantasy pictures spewed out by the media. The effect of sexual liberation has far from liberated women. Rather it has become a snare into which women are led for the greater benefit of men's sexual gratification and irresponsibility.

Islam, in contrast, commands humans to marry, which is first and foremost an act of piety. Marriage further brings benefits of emotional and sexual gratification, cohesion between families, and social stability.

> And among His Signs is this, that He created for you mates from among yourselves, that you may dwell in tranquillity with them, and He has put love and mercy between your (hearts): verily in that are Signs for those who reflect.
>
> *[al-Rum 30:21]*

> It is He Who created you from a single person, and made his mate of like nature, in order that he might dwell with her (in love)...
>
> *[al-A'raf 7:189]*

> And Allah has made for you mates (and companions) of your own nature, and made for you, out of them, sons and daughters and grandchildren, and provided for you sustenance of the best: will they then believe in vain things, and be ungrateful for Allah's favours?
>
> *[al-Nahl 16 : 72]*

(See also *al-Baqarah* 2:187; *al-Shura* 42:11; *al-Nisa'* 4:1)

There are feminists who advocate and eagerly anticipate technological advances that will replace the woman's role in childbearing. No doubt their wait will be in vain, because even if such technology were to be developed, it would surely be in the hands of men. Instead of becoming liberated, women would be rendered useless and be placed at the mercy of males.

The feminists see the main causes of women's oppression as lying in the political and legal system, especially English common law which has its roots in Christianity (religion in general); marriage, childbearing and the family. Islam's response to these concerns may be summed up as follows:

1. The rise of feminism in the West was due to the high level of social, legal, political and economic suppression of women. The first suffragette movement in Britain was established to address the political and economic inequality suffered by women, especially those who were married. Throughout the twentieth century, women have fought in the home, the workplace and the street for equal legal and political status. Women in Islam, unlike their Western counterparts, did not need to embark upon any such campaign. Every individual in Islam, male or female, is considered to be an independent person who is responsible and accountable for his or her own actions and is answerable only to Allah. A Muslim woman has equal status in business; if she commits a crime, her punishment is no more or less than that of a man. If compensation is due to her, she is dealt with on equal terms with a man in a similar case. Marriage does not affect her legal status, her property or earnings, or even her name. Thus the demands of the Western women, which have been only partially won after much bitter struggle, were handed on a plate, as it were, to the Muslim women, fourteen hundred years ago.

2. Feminist fears surrounding marriage, childbearing and family as a means of oppression have been discussed in the previous chapter. The following points may be noted by way of summary:

   a) Marriage in Islam is a means of obtaining contentment, but if a union is not successful, then the marriage can and should be dissolved. The Qur'an commends marriage in several places (see *al-Nisa'* 4:1; *al-Nur* 32-33; *al-Rum* 30:21). For a Muslim who has freely accepted Islam and is a sincere believer, marriage entails rights and responsibilities, but is not seen as restrictive. Individuals who enter wedlock must comply with Qur'anic injunctions; any failure to do so brings the threat of divine punishment in the Hereafter. Professor Lois Lamya' al-Faruqi listed the purpose and benefits of marriage as follows:[1]

- For an individual who has freely submitted to Islam, marriage is an act of piety.
- Marriage is a mechanism for the moral and mutual benefit of controlling sexual behaviour and procreation.
- Marriage provides a stable atmosphere for the rearing of children.
- Marriage ensures crucial economic benefits for women during their childrearing years.
- Marriage provides emotional gratification for both men and women.
- Marriage acts as a protection from sin and as an interdependent institution.

b) In Islam, children are seen as a bounty from Allah, and their birth is a joyous occasion. According to the *sunnah*, the newborn infant should be given a good name on the seventh day; his or her head should be shaved and the weight of the hair in gold or silver should be given in charity as a sign of gratitude to Allah. It is also recommended to sacrifice a lamb and distribute its meat among the poor. The Qur'an explicitly states that children should not be seen as reducing wealth or curtailing one's freedom, and any acts such as abortion or infanticide are strongly condemned. (See *al-An'am* 6:140, 150; *al-Isra'* 17:31).

Children are considered to be the apple of our eyes. However, the Qur'an also warns against becoming unduly proud and investing vanity and false hopes of security in one's children (see *Al 'Imran* 3:14; *al-Anfal* 8:28; *al-Tawbah* 9:69; *al-Kahf* 18:46; *al-Mu'minun* 23:55; *Saba'* 34:35; *al-Hadid* 57:20; *al-Taghabun* 64:15; *al-Qalam* 68:14)

---

[1] Prof. Lois Lamya al Faruqi. *Women Muslim Society & Islam*. Indianapolis. American Trust Publication. 1988.

c) According to the Islamic view, the family extends beyond the "nuclear" circle of father, mother and children to include grandparents, uncles, aunts, nieces, nephews, and all their offspring. Rather than being a burden and crushing a woman's independence, the extended family should act as a support and means of building confidence. The Qur'an repeatedly enjoins kind treatment of kinsfolk and orphans (see *al-Baqarah* 2:177; *al-Anfal* 8:41; *al-Nahl* 16:90; *al-Isra'* 17:26).

In the light of Islamic teaching, some of the advantages of the extended family may be outlined as follows:[1]

- Family members provide diverse company and intellectual stimulation, which fosters a broadly-based environment in which children and adults may grow and develop.
- Family members are there to provide support, sympathy and advice at times of trouble.
- Quarrels may be quickly resolved as family members act as mediators and provide counsel.
- Parenting problems are reduced as different family members assist in childrearing.
- The extended family can assist in matchmaking, thus eliminating any perceived need for "singles clubs" or marriage agencies.
- Working parents need not feel guilty about leaving their children, as they will be cared for by family members; this provides ideal support for working women.
- Tragedies such as divorce will not be quite so devastating because the peer group within the extended family will cushion the blow somewhat.
- Detrimental behaviour towards oneself or one's marriage will be less likely because the peer group within the extended family will oppose it.
- Far from being a burden to women, as the feminists fear, the family is in fact a great asset for the modern woman.[2]

---

[1] *Ibid.*
[2] *Ibid.*

3. Western women who see religion as the cause of their oppression are diametrically opposed to Muslim women who have seen the teachings of Islam and the way of the Prophet ﷺ as the greatest means of emancipation and attainment of equal status with men.[1] Islam has given the Muslim woman a status which is far above that to which Western women aspire. So Islam has become a haven for today's educated, thinking women. Muslim women consider their religion to be their greatest friend, not the enemy as their counterparts in other societies see it.

At this point, the practical situation of some women in Muslim societies today need to be addressed. It is an unfortunate and shameful fact that many rights which have been afforded to Muslim women by Allah have been denied to them by men. This is largely due to the fact that many Muslim men have embraced Western culture, extracted what suits them, and used this to oppress women. Many girls are denied the opportunity of an education and career, their marriage rights are ignored, their inheritance dues are consumed and their fate in the event of a divorce is deplorable. If we are to restore social order – and for the Muslim that means Allah's order – then Muslim men, with the aid of competent, sincere Muslim scholars, need to implement the whole *shari'ah* and apply it equally to both males and females. Modesty and the dress-code, along with a thorough education about all the issues involved, need to be implemented and applied to both men and women.

However, even with the shortcomings that exist today, what Islam has to offer women is far better than any other options open to them. The comments made by Western women who embrace Islam are very interesting. A British researcher, Harfiyah Ball, interviewed a number of new Muslims and reported the following comments:

- "[Before I accepted Islam] I had no feeling of purpose, no sense of direction, proportion, perspective. My life was unsettled, no guidance, no certainty, no proper aim, pointless and empty".
- "Islam has given me all the answers to my questions. I am at home with the universe. I am at peace and content. I have my

---

[1] *Ibid.*

guiding light to follow - Allah. I seek no more than to continue to be guided by Allah and to surrender wholly to His will. *This has the effect of ushering one above pomp, idols and intermediaries. You only do what pleases Allah and that frees you from worldly demands*". (Italics mine).

- "No one seemed to care about the family, friends or strangers. Friendship with people was not close. Emotions were superficial, e.g. relationships with women formed only between boyfriends. I felt pressure from society to leave home and live independently".
- "I was lonely".
- "My girlfriends were always looking for boyfriends; all I wanted was friends".

Although there have been many improvements in the situation of Western women and the model of Western liberated women has been promoted worldwide, many Western women have expressed dissatisfaction about attitudes towards women in their own societies. Women feel that they are expected to fend for themselves, to compete for their survival with men. Their society expects them to be self-sufficient as well as glamorous and domesticated.[1] Many other pressures in Western society have seen the feminist bandwagon grind to a halt as women come to realise its impracticality and the restrictions it places on women's freedom and happiness. Young intellectual women have found that feminism has failed them, and they are now looking towards more prudent, sustainable teachings, such as Islam. In "The new Victorians: a young woman's challenge to the old feminist order", the author Denfeld states: "Feminism is bogged down in an extremist moral and spiritual crusade that has little to do with women's lives and it has climbed out on an academic limb that is all but inaccessible". Her sentiments are not surprising since surveys in the USA have shown that whereas in 1986, 56% of American women considered themselves to be feminists, by 1992, only 29% described themselves as such.[2]

---

[1]   Harfiyah Ball, *Why British women embrace Islam*, Volcano Press. Leicester UK.
[2]   *Gulf News*, 26/5/1995.

As the feigned concerns of the feminist are becoming apparent. The thinking women are waking up and searching for a more prudent ethos to conduct their way of life. It is greatly regrettably that after one hundred years of feminist dictates, women are as worst off in real terms as a century ago. Poverty is increasingly a women's problem. Women are made to fend for themselves and their families. In certain areas of Britain one in three families[1] are headed by a woman on her own (compared with one in two hundred headed by men alone). Although English women represent 50% of undergraduates only a negligible few ever reach the top of their career. Western women suffering from mental illness and depression is higher than their male counterparts. The woman in the west has been demeaned so much that her body is considered a public object available for man's gratification by casually 'watching girl's go by' to sale in pornography, or as a sensual object for advertisers to use in promoting merchandise and prostitution. The consequences of all these is that the woman in the west is portrayed as an object of entertainment, valued for her beauty and a work horse suppling the male with sensual gratification and the capitalist system with surplus profit. The Western woman has been *short changed* of her integrity, intellect and personality.

If the feminists are genuinely interested in the emancipation of women, they need to challenge the present Western system by uniting women and men of all races under the umbrella of a logical and sustainable ideology that can be applied equally across the East/West and North/South divides and address the universal human concerns of child-care, equal opportunities, pregnancy rights, protection and education. One need look no further than the principles and teachings of Islam, which offer security, legal and financial freedom, emancipation from sexual and physical harassment, and equality of status. Islam has been portrayed as a misogynist villain in the West, because it threatens the existing social order of bourgeoisie, monetary ideology, sexual deviancy and oppression. Islam faces the opposition from parties with vested interests who have a stake in denying women express their true identity. The greatest tragedy of Western women,

---

[1] Social Trends 1996.

especially those in the feminist movement, is their lack of aspiration: they have aspired only to be like men, instead of re-evaluating and reclaiming what women are best at. The heritage of women has been devalued by Western men and capitalist society. It is up to women to look to the principles and way of life that credits them for their being. This can only be found in Islam.

BIBLIOGRAPHY

Translations of the Holy Qur'an:

Ali, A. Yusuf (trans.). *The Holy Qur'an*. Madina: Islamic Propagation Centre International, 1946.

Daryabadi, Maulana Abdul Majid (trans.). *The Holy Qur'an*. Lucknow, India. Academy of Research & Publications. 1981.

Usmani, Allama Shabbir (trans.). *The Holy Qur'an*. (English trans. by Mohammad Ashfaq Ahmad). New Delhi, India: Idara Isha'at-E-Diniyat, 1992.

Ahadith:

Abu Dawood. *Sunnan Abu Dawood*, trans. Prof. Ahmad Hasan. Pub. SH Muhammad Ashraf, Lahore, Pakistan. 1984.

al-Nawawi, Imam. *Riyadh al-Saliheen*. Trans. S. M. Madni Abbasi, Karachi, Pakistan: International Islamic Publishers, 1991.

Bukhari, Imam. *Sahih al-Bukhari*. Trans. Dr. Muhammad Muhsin Khan, Kazi Publication, Lahore, Pakistan. 1984.

Hasan, Prof. Ahmad. *Sunan Abi Dawood*. Lahore, Pakistan: Sh. Muhammad Ashraf, 1984.

James Robson, (trans), *Mishkat al -Masabih*. Lahore, Pakistan. Sh. Muhammad Ashraf. 1994.

Muslim, Imam. *Sahih Muslim*. Trans. Abdul Hamid Siddiqi. New Delhi: Kitab Bhavan,1979.

Tirmidhi, Imam. *Sunan al-Tirmidhi*. (Urdu translation). Karachi, Pakistan: Idara Ishat,1985.

Government publications:

Canadian Client Custom Services, Health Statistic Division.

U.K. Annual Abstract Statistics 1996.

U.K. Criminal Statistics England & Wales 1996.

U.K. Office of Population survey 1993.

U.K. Social Trends 1996.

U.S. Census Bureau – 'Household and Family Characteristics, March 1994.

U.S. Census Bureau – 'Household and Family Characteristics, March 1995.

U.S. Statistical Abstract of the United States 1994.

U.S. National Centre for Health Statistics. Health, United States, 1995.

Other sources:

Archer, Leonie, *et al. Women in ancient societies.* London: Macmillan Press. 1994.

Ball, Harifayah. *Why British women embrace Islam.* Leicester, UK: Muslim Youth Education Council, 1987.

Banks, Olive. *Becoming a feminist.* Brighton: Wheatsheaf Books, 1986.

————. *Faces of feminism.* Oxford: Martin Robertson, 1981.

Barrett, Michele. *Women's oppression today.* London: Verso, 1980.

Bashier, Zakaria. *Muslim women in the midst of change.* Leicester: The Islamic Foundation, 1980.

Bemat, Maulana Mufti Ahmed. *The Muslim women.* Madani Kutubkhana.

Boucher, David. *The feminist challenge: the movement for women's liberation in Britain and America.* London: Macmillan Press, 1983.

Burton, Clare. *Subordination: feminism and social theory.* Sydney: George Allen & Unwin, 1989.

Deckard, Barbara Sinclair. *The women's movement: political, socioeconomic and psychological issues.* New York: University of California, Pub. Harper & Row. 1983.

Delderfield, Eric. *Kings and Queens of England & Britain.* London: David & Charles, 1990.

Doi, Abdur Rahman I. *Women in Shariah.* London: Ta-Ha, 1989.

Evans, Judith. *Feminist theory today – an introduction to second wave feminism.* London: Sage Publications, 1995.

Ferguson, Ann. *Sexual democracy : women, oppression and revolution.* Boulder, Colarado: Westview Press, 1991.

Firestone, Shulmith. *The dialectic of sex : the case for feminist revolution.* New York: William Morrow & Company, inc., 1970.

Freeman, Hugh. *Progress in mental health : Proceedings of the seventh international congress on mental health.* London: Churchill. 1968.

Graham, Hilary. *Hardship and health in women's lives.* New York: Harvester Wheatsheaf, 1993.

Gunew, Sneja. *Feminist knowledge: critique and construction.* London: Routledge, 1990.

Hakim, Hazrat. *The status of women in Islam.* Azadville, South Africa: Jet Printers, 1990.

Hamid, Abdul Wahid. *Islam – the natural way.* London: Muslim Education & Literary Services (MELS), 1989.

Khan, M. Rafiq. *Life and work of Imam Bukhari.* Varanasi, India: Idarat ul Buhoos Jamia Shafia, 1984.

Lerner, Gerda. *The creation of patriarchy.* New York: Oxford University Press, 1986.

Lorber, Judith & Susan Farrell. *The social construction of gender.* Newbury Park, California: Sage Publications, 1991.

Ragie, Maulana Zahier. *Kitabun nikah.* Azadville, South Africa: Madrasa Arabia Islamia. South Africa, 1992.

Richards, Janet Radcliffe. *The sceptical feminist.* London: Routledge & Kegan Paul,1980.

Stanley, Liz & Sue Wise. *Breaking out again.* London: Routledge, 1993.

Suleiman, Rubin. *The female body in Western culture: contemporary perspectives.* Cambridge, Massachusetts: Harvard University Press, 1986.

Thanwi, Maulana Ashraf Ali. *Behisti zewar.* Delhi, India: Dini Book Depot, 1987.

Tong, Rosemarie. *Feminist thought: a comprehensive introduction.* London: Routledge, 1989.

Wolf, Naomi. *The beauty myth.* London: Vintage, 1991.

Young, Kimball. *Isn't one wife enough?* New York: Henry Holt & Co., 1954.

Zaretsky, Eli. *Capitalism, the family and personal life.* New York: Harper & Row, 1976.

Further Reading:

Afza, Nazhat and Khurshid Ahmed. The position of women in Islam. Kuwait: Islamic Book Publishers, 1982.

Aijaz, Zakir S. Muslim children – how to bring up children? Karachi, Pakistan: International Islamic Publishers, 1991.

Abdalati, Hammudah. The family structure in Islam. Indianapolis: American Trust Publications, 1977.

Azami, Maulana Majaz. Guidance for a Muslim wife. Azadville, South Africa: Madrasah Arabia Islamia, 1990.

Badawi, Dr. Jamal. The status of women in Islam. Birmingham, UK: Islamic Propagation Centre International.

Beck, Lois & Nikki Keddie (eds.). Women in the Muslim world. Cambridge, Massachusetts: Harvard University Press, 1978.

Bouhdiba, Abdelwahab (translated by Alan Sheridan). Sexuality in Islam. London: Routledge & Kegan Paul, 1985.

Deckard, Barbara Sinclair. The women's movement. New York: University of California, 1979.

Dewmark, Florence. Who discriminates against women? Beverly Hills: Sage Publications, 1974.

Doi, Abdur Rahman. Women in Qur'an and Sunnah. London: Ta-Ha, 1990.

Doi, Abdur Rahman. Women in Shari'ah. Ta-Ha. 1989.

Engineer, Asghar Ali. The rights of women in Islam. London: C.Hurst & Co., 1992.

Faruqi, Lois Lamya. Women, Muslim society and Islam. Indianapolis: American Trust Publications, 1988.

Frazer, Elizabeth et al. (eds.). Ethics: a feminist reader. Oxford: Blackwell, 1992.

Friedman, Susan Stanford. A woman's guide to therapy: Prentice, 1979.

Haykal, Muhammad Husayn. The life of Muhammad. Indianapolis: American Trust Publications, 1976.

Hewitt, Ibrahim B. What does Islam say about...? London: The Muslim Education Trust, 1993.

Iqbal, Safia. Women and Islamic law. Delhi, India: Pub. Adam , 1988.

Iqbal, Sufi Muhammad. Forty ahadith on the virtues of women. Leicester: Ilmi Publications, 1990

Ishaq, Ibn. The life of Muhammad (translated by A. Guillaume). Karachi: Oxford University, 1955.

Ismail, Maulana Abdullah. Awake! Young women of Islam. 1994.

Karolia, Maulana Muhammad. The rights of women. Azadville, South Africa: Pub. Madrasah Arabia Islamia, 1994.

Khan, Sharif Ahmed. Modesty and chastity in Islam. Kuwait: Islamic Book Publishers, 1982.

Malik, Fida Hussain. Wives of the Holy Prophet (PBUH). Delhi, India: Taj [publisher?], 1952.

Miller, Leo. John Milton among the polygamophiles. New York, USA: Loewenthal Press, 1974.

Mitchell, Juliet. Women – the longest revolution. New York: Pantheon Books, 1984.

Murata, Sachiko. The Tao of Islam. Albany, New York: State University of New York, 1992.

Palmer, Phyllis. Domesticity and dirt: housewives and domestic servants in the United States 1920-1945. Philadelphia: Temple University Press, 1989.

Russell, Bertrand. A history of Western philosophy. London: Counterpoint, 1946.

Smith, J.R. & Smith, L.G. Beyond polygamy. London: Johns

Hopkins University Press, 1974.

Spelman, Elizabeth. Inessential women: problems of exclusion in feminist thought. London: Womens Press, 1990.

Suleiman, Rubin. The female body in Western culture. Cambridge, Massachusetts: Harvard University Press, 1986.

Tavard, George Henry. Women in Christian tradition. London: Notre Dame, 1973.

Utas, Bo. Women in Islamic society: social attitudes and historical perspectives. London: Curzon Press, 1983.

GLOSSARY OF TERMS

Ayah   With reference to this book the word means individual units or verses of the Qur'an.

Deen   Refers to the way of life conducted in the manner advocated by Allah. Thus in Islam deen consists of living in total submission to the will of Allah.

Hadith   The record of what the Prophet Muhammad said, did and approved.

'iddah   The waiting period a women is required to observe because of divorce or death of her husband.

Jahiliyyah   Denotes the period of ignorance before Prophet Muhammad's time and also the views which reject Allah's guidance.

Khul   Signifies a woman securing release from a marriage contract.

AH   'After Hijri' - Islamic calendar beginning from the day the Prophet Muhammad migrated (made hijrat) to Medina from Mecca (both in present day Saudi Arabia).

CE   'Christian Era' – Present day calendar based on Christianity.

Qadi   A Judge who resides in an Islamic court.

Sheikh   In this book, the title is awarded to individuals who are scholars of Islam.

Mufti   An individual who is versed in the Islamic jurisprudence.

ﷺ   Used at the end of Prophet Muhammad's name. It means– May Allah bless him and be pleased with him.

رضي الله عنه   Placed after the name of Prophet Muhammad's companion. May Allah be pleased with her or him.

Hijab   A term used to describe the female dress code according to the Islamic way. Nowadays the scarf to cover the head, face and outer cloak is referred to as the Hijab.

Allah	The proper Arabic name for God.
Islam	This is the religion preached by all the Prophets - from Adam and finalised with Muhammad. It literally means to submit to the will of Allah.
Qur'an	This is the book which represent the verbatum word of Allah revealed through Muhammad. This book has never been altered in any way or form since the time of it's revelation.
Talaq	The term used to divorce; it also means divorce.
Zina	Adultery
bid'i	An innovation in religion; heresy.
Sunnah	Those things which the Prophet Muhammad enjoined on his followers.
Injeel	This is the original book promulgated by Jesus. It does not represent the new or old testament nor the four Gospels which have been written by men after the time of Jesus.
Tawrat	This was the original scripture 'or laws' promulgated by Mosses.

Index

90, 92, 94, 96, 99, 101, 119, 120

M

Mental illness 26, 27, 91, 102
Modesty 29, 36, 56, 57, 58, 59, 119

N

New Muslims 100

O

Oppression 6, 8, 10, 12, 16, 17, 18, 24, 25, 31, 36, 65,
    67, 69, 70, 71, 72, 74, 75, 76, 77, 78, 80, 84, 85, 86, 87,
    88, 90, 92, 93, 97, 100, 102, 105, 106

P

Patriarchy 78, 79, 80, 106
Playboy 85, 89
Police 21, 23
Polygyny 47, 49
Pornographic films 28
Pornographic magazines 28
Pornography 28, 56, 87

Q

Qur'anic References
    al 'Imran 4, 33, 98
    al-Ahqaf 93, 94
    al-Ahzab 32, 51, 60
    al-An'am 98
    al-A'raf 38, 96
    al-Baqarah 3, 38, 43, 54, 94, 96, 99
    al-Hashr 2
    al-Ikhlas 2
    al-Isra 57, 98, 99
    al-Nahl 33, 35, 39, 96, 99
    al-Naml 83
    al-Nisa 38, 39, 43, 48, 49, 53, 55, 61, 62, 96, 97